JIMMY DEMARET

THE SWING'S THE THING

by
John Companiotte

Clock Tower Press
Ann Arbor, MI

Clock Tower Press, LLC
3622 W. Liberty
Ann Arbor, MI 48103
www.clocktowerpress.com

Printed and bound in Canada.

10 9 8 7 6 5 4 3 2 1

Library of Congress Cataloging-in-Publication Data

Companiotte, John.
 Jimmy Demaret : the swing's the thing / by John Companiotte.
    p. cm.
 ISBN 1-932202-10-2
 1. Demaret, Jimmy. 2. Golfers—United States—Biography. I. Title.
GV994.D46C66 2004
796.352'092—dc22

                                                        2003020320

For my wife, Catherine.

CONTENTS

FOREWORD

By Jack Burke

Jimmy Demaret and I traveled the PGA Tour together, played golf together (including being teammates on the victorious 1951 Ryder Cup squad), started a golf club together, and shared an office during the years we developed and ran Champions Golf Club. My father had hired Jimmy to work at River Oaks when Jimmy was still a teenager, and Champions, our joint venture, was his primary professional activity for the last 25 years of his life. I used to joke that the Burkes had been employing Jimmy all his life. Jimmy's comeback was that he had been baby-sitting me all his life, starting with his time at River Oaks.

We had so many good times together that it is difficult to focus on just a few. Jimmy's wit and general good nature made every day of working with him enjoyable. The very day that Jimmy died, which happened at Champions, he was on his way to get a haircut. The last thing he said to me was that he hoped the woman who cut his hair "slept well last night."

Jimmy was well known as one of the most successful players ever on the PGA Tour and for his endless supply of one-liners. Less well known were his talents in other areas. He was a good pilot, a good singer, and a good business partner. After the club's founding in the late 1950s, Champions rapidly established itself as one of the premier clubs not only in Houston and the Southwest, but anywhere golf is played. Jimmy's contribution helped it reach this stature. His easy ability to relate to the club members, the staff, and eventually the many people involved in hosting the events that came to Champions, was an invaluable asset.

There was no one like Jimmy Demaret. Golf has lacked some fun and spontaneity since his passing. But he left a great legacy to the game by helping promote the PGA Tour in its early years, by playing some great golf during his days on Tour, and by giving back to the game whenever he could. Most importantly, he was my good friend and I still miss him.

INTRODUCTION

By Ben Crenshaw

Every young touring pro today has men like Jimmy Demaret to thank for the wonderful opportunities they have. In 1940 Jimmy enjoyed six tournament wins, which included the Masters. After winning the Masters he went back to Houston as fast as he could to make sure he didn't lose his job as a club pro. Do you think times were tough? At that time, the players were hoping they could win tournaments so that they could get a country club's professional post. How different it is today.

Jimmy Demaret had a wonderful pair of hands and forearms. They didn't call him Popeye for nothing. I loved to watch him walk into the ball, with that familiar couple of no-nonsense waggles, and then—crack—there would go the ball on a low flying trajectory. He could work marvels with a heavy wind and like every great golfer, any golf shot to him was like an art form.

What an attitude to go along with these great physical blessings! He once told me to try and relax a little more when playing. He said, "If things started to go a little sour for me, and I started to drop shots, I thought, 'Hell, they're not going to put me in jail even if I shoot 80,' and then pretty soon I'd be a couple under par again." Golf was fun for Jimmy. He'd also say, "The idea is to save shots; we can't all hit the greens, so let's work a little harder on our short game." Hear that everyone? Including me!

Champions Golf Club, which he co-owned with Jackie Burke, is a great place to learn about the game. I have never seen a more successful golf club. Every square inch of Champions is an extension of these great men's feelings and understanding of the game. It all works and functions and flows just as it should. Along with two great courses, the clubhouse is something to behold. Tasteful, comfortable surroundings are very dear to the golfer once the round is finished, and Champions locker room has been the scene of many famous Demaret-Burke court holdings. On more than one occasion Jimmy has challenged many people to a match of one-legged golf, in which you would play as best you know how and he would hit the ball off either leg, but all the while, on his backswing, you could tell him which leg to hit from!

A more colorful player or personality has never set foot on the Tour. Jimmy's clothes were something else: pink, canary yellow, and robin's egg blue when others wore gray, navy, and brown. He always said when someone whistled at him, he just whistled back with a big smile. And what a smile he had. When he met you, he'd give you that handshake and a smile and a laugh that made you feel warm inside. I suppose there are two lines in Rudyard Kipling's poem *If* that describe Jimmy Demaret well—"If you can talk with crowds and keep your virtue/Or walk with Kings—nor lose the common touch," yes, Jimmy got along with everyone. Caddies, help around the club, movie stars, and rich folks, everybody was Demaret's friend. Let us remember him for his wonderful contributions to golf, that great smile of his, and the feeling that we were about to have fun. He'd like it that way.

—Adapted from an article written by Ben Crenshaw
for the program for the 1984 Liberty Mutual
Legends of Golf held at Onion Creek Club

Jimmy Demaret

The Swing's the Thing

Jimmy Demaret as a young man. (courtesy of Charles Newman)

THE MAKING OF A CHAMPION

"A Human Rainbow in Action"

◆ ◆ ◆

Three Masters victories are enough to establish Jimmy Demaret as one of the best golfers ever to play the game. Winning one major is confirmation of a player's ability, focus, and composure under pressure. Occasionally a golfer puts it all together for one week, which is frequently the highlight of his or her career, a justifiably respectable highlight. Winning two majors makes a more significant statement about courage and skill. Without a doubt, only the very best golfers have collected trophies from three majors.

Jimmy Demaret was in that select group, and his total of 31 wins on the PGA Tour still ranks him among the top 15 players in total wins, more than 40 years after he stopped actively competing. He won tournaments from San Francisco to Miami, Havana to Argentina, frequently singing while he strolled the fairways. He had a golf game that traveled well and a personality that made him friends wherever he went. As a host of *Shell's Wonderful World of Golf* during the 1960s, crisscrossing the globe for matches featuring the world's best players, he continued to entertain whenever he set foot on a golf course. He left behind unforgettable remarks such as, "Golf and sex are about the only things you can enjoy without being good at them."

Jimmy Demaret was as good an example of the American dream as can be found. Born to modest circumstances, he developed his skills as a golfer into a level of play that earned him a place among the best. He befriended movie stars, politicians, businessmen, astronauts, and thousands of golf fans. He succeeded as a partner in one of the great golf clubs, Champions Golf Club in Houston, while enjoying success as an endorser of a broad range of products. He was a pilot, he contributed to golf course designs, and he helped found an event that inspired the PGA Seniors Tour. He was the single biggest influence in golfers wearing more comfortable and colorful clothing. He accomplished all this and enjoyed the regard of his fellow players.

"Of all the guys on the tour, I think Demaret was more well-liked than anybody, by the pros and the fans both," said Sam Snead. "He was a wonderful guy." Nearly 40 years before Snead's comments, sportswriter Grantland Rice said the same thing about Demaret: "There certainly isn't another fellow in golf who is better liked, both by players and galleries."

John O'Brien Demaret, Jimmy's father, was a "carpenter, roofer, house painter, and general building tradesman," as Demaret described him in the book *My Partner, Ben Hogan*. Born May 10, 1910 in Houston, James Newton Demaret credited helping his father mix paints as the origin of his fascination with colors, leading to his designation as "a human rainbow in action," as Rice described him. His mother, Mary (Lila Mae Winkler), was a sufficiently devout Catholic that she rode the bus so that she could attend Mass, and Demaret revered her memory all his life. With nine children in the family, five of them boys, work began at an early age, with most of the boys holding paper routes. The children in order of birth were Mary, Lyman, Milton, Jimmy, Juanita, Al, Jane, Leona, and Mahlon.

Frances Trimble in an article for *Golf Houston* in July 2001 described Demaret's family background. "In 1910, the year Jimmy was born, the Demaret family lived on Center Street, west of downtown. John Demaret's brother, Patrick, a telephone company lineman, lived nearby with wife Myrtle. Another Demaret brother named Dave, Amanda Winkler (Lila Mae's mother), and her son Milton, also lived in the neighborhood."

Jimmy's sister Jane later remembered that her mother could not keep light bulbs in the house because the boys were always swinging golf clubs indoors. Seven years younger than Jimmy, she turned out to be a fine golfer herself, winning the club championship for women at Riverbend in Houston six times.

The year Jimmy Demaret was born the British Open celebrated its Golden Jubilee (1860–1910). James Braid won his fifth title in the event that year, and Alex Smith won his second U.S. Open, beating his brother Macdonald Smith and Johnny McDermott in a three-way play-off. Noted golf course designer A.W. Tillinghast finished 25th in the U.S. Open in 1910, though his fame came later from designing Winged Foot, Baltusrol, and other championship layouts. Charles "Chick" Evans Jr., who would establish a caddie scholarship program that would be named in honor of him, won the Western Open in Chicago, an event that Demaret would win when it was played in Houston in 1940. Also in 1910, Arthur F. Knight of Schenectady, New York obtained a patent for a seamed, tubular steel golf shaft, but it would be over 20 years before steel-shafted clubs took over from hickory.

Houston in 1910 had a population of a little over 100,000 including the city's suburbs, making it the largest city in Texas. Several factors contributed to Houston growing by 1930 to a population of 300,000. In 1914 the Houston Ship Channel opened, which would ultimately contribute to Houston being within the top three ports in the United States for shipping volume. A decade before Demaret was born, on the morning of January 10, 1901 the Lucas gusher, near Beaumont, Texas, was the start of what was known as the Spindletop oil discovery. That led to a major oil industry being centered in Houston and south Texas. The associated petrochemicals industry became one of the two largest concentrations of that industry in America. Prior to the growth of the shipping and oil industries Houston had been a center for the cotton, rice, lumber, cattle, and other agricultural businesses of Texas. The city would grow to become one of the four largest in America by the 1970s.

Rice Institute, which became Rice University, was founded in Houston in 1912. The school was one of the founding members of the Southwest Conference (SWC) in 1914, and the golf team was conference champions in 1929, 1930, and 1939, a year that Demaret served as the team's coach.

Several businessmen from Houston became prominent at the national level. Howard Hughes was raised in Houston. At age 20 in 1924 he inherited the Hughes Tool Company, which cleared "$60 million a year after taxes at a time when $60 million had the buying power of $600 million by 1986 dollars," as stated by Marguerite Johnson in her book *Houston: The Unknown City, 1836–1946*. Hughes played to a two handicap at Houston Country Club. Jesse H. Jones was one of the prominent builders in Houston, having built 30 commercial structures by the mid-1920s. He helped attract the 1928 Democratic National Convention to the city and he later served as secretary of commerce in Franklin D. Roosevelt's administration. The Jesse H. Jones School of Management at Rice University, whose finance program was named number one in the U.S. by *The Economist* in 2002, was named for Jones.

"Golf in Houston was in a pretty primitive stage when I got my first introduction to it," Demaret said 45 years later. "The only course here was Houston Country Club, and then a nine-hole sand green course was put in at Camp Logan during World War I."

While walking past the Camp Logan army hospital golf course near his home at around age seven, Demaret witnessed golf for the first time, watching some of the patients hitting golf balls (according to the form he filled out in 1975 for his induction into the Texas Sports Hall of Fame). He later recalled his first experience with golf. "A bunch of us kids were playing baseball near Camp Logan one morning," he said, "when a Major Stinson interrupted our game and told us he needed some caddies at the golf course.

"We got a dime a bag. We were all seven or eight years old and we'd never seen that much money. When I was nine, I was the caddie master, meaning all I had to do was round up caddies." Children were able to carry a golfer's clubs because no more than six clubs made up a set at the time, contained in a small canvas bag. This mix of clubs would be a couple of woods, a mid-iron, a mid-mashie, a niblick, and a putter.

He was also selling newspapers around this time, but golf quickly captured his interest and soon Demaret was caddying at the nine-hole course. His older brother Lyman had preceded him as a caddy at the course, so he must have had someone to give him a bit of instruction about what to do and how to conduct himself.

Demaret could later recall the first golf club he owned. "It was an old wooden-shafted niblick [9-iron]," he remembered. "When school was out in the afternoon, I'd hit balls along the way as I walked to the golf course. The kids looked at me like they thought I was crazy. A lot of them had never seen a golf club, and actually didn't know what it was."

By age 11 Demaret had won his first caddie tournament at Camp Logan. Then he ventured to Hermann Park, a municipal facility in Houston, where he worked for several years, spending time buffing golf clubs, and making and repairing the wooden shafts of the clubs used by golfers at that time. Another civic leader, George H. Hermann, had donated land for Hermann Park, which in 1922 opened an 18-hole golf course designed by a Houston stockbroker and supporter of golf, George V. Roten and the engineer David M. Duller. The park is located across from Rice University on South Main Street.

In his book *My Partner, Ben Hogan,* Demaret described his work at Hermann Park: "People sometimes ask me today how I obtained my wrist and forearm development. The answer is simple—from my weekly chore of buffing 350 sets of clubs that had been hacked and chipped over the weekend by the members. Also, I was a member of the last generation of golf pros that served a rugged apprenticeship making and mending those wooden shafts, just before the mass factory production of clubs began. I was listed as an 'apprentice clubmaker' at Hermann Park and was able to fill the job because my father had schooled me well in the handling of tools. I learned the techniques of making and mending the hickory shafts thoroughly, and most any hour of the day I could be found pressing them against the shop lathe."

Years later the head professional at Memorial Park, Robie Williams, who worked with Demaret at Hermann Park, remembered

Demaret from his early days, giving him credit for being more serious about golf than people appreciated. "Fans don't realize how much Jimmy worked at the game in his early years," said Williams in 1961. "At heart, I would say he is a more serious competitor than Ben Hogan; he just doesn't use the same methods.

"Jimmy has a true love for golf. In fact, he loves the game more than anyone I've ever known. He's lucky to accept it as a game. Lucky isn't the word there, on second thought, as I don't believe the word luck enters into the Demaret story. He would have been a success at anything he undertook."

Williams recalled the days when Jimmy was a young pro at Hermann Park. "Golly, there's no telling how much he cost the city, hitting balls off the side porch when it was raining. He must have worn out three sets of flooring."

According to Demaret's account of his early years in his book on Hogan, he then spent time at Golfcrest Country Club and Houston's Colonial Country Club, which became Brae Burn Country Club in the 1930s. Another public golf course in Houston that Demaret frequented all his life was Memorial Park Golf Course, whose present design was completed by John Bredemus in the 1930s. Bredemus was later notable for doing the original design work on Ft. Worth's Colonial Country Club and other courses around Texas, including Brae Burn in 1927, where Demaret would become head professional in 1936.

The land for Memorial Park became available when Camp Logan was dismantled and the land was put up for sale. One parcel of 873 acres and another one of 630 acres were combined to create the park. When Memorial Park Golf Course was first constructed, just one recreation amenity in a park stretching over 1,503 acres, Harvey Penick claimed it was "the best muny in the country," a "muny" being a municipal course. Remarkably for the era, when Memorial was built it measured over 7,000 yards from the back tees, not all of which were used even for tournaments. Memorial first hosted the PGA Tour's Houston Open in 1947. Brae Burn hosted the event in 1950, then it returned to Memorial in 1951, where it was played through

1963. The course had a complete renovation during 1994 and 1995. Memorial Park Golf Course now has a lighted driving range, putting and chipping greens, a new clubhouse facility, and a golf museum created from the original clubhouse structure.

Bredemus also influenced Cedar Crest in Dallas getting the opportunity to host the 1927 PGA Championship. Earlier in his life he had been one of the first members of The PGA when it was chartered in 1916. Born in 1884, Bredemus attended Princeton and graduated with a degree in civil engineering in 1912. An excellent athlete, Bredemus in 1908 won the AAU National All-Around competition in track and field. In the same competition in 1912, Bredemus finished runner-up to Jim Thorpe. Then in 1913 Thorpe was stripped of his medals from both the 1912 Olympics and the AAU event because he previously had played semipro baseball. Bredemus as runner-up was sent the AAU medals. For the rest of his life people mistakenly believed that Bredemus had possession of Thorpe's Olympic medals.

Another person involved in design work with John Bredemus during the 1930s was Ralph Plummer. He was hired as head golf professional at Galveston Municipal while Bredemus was constructing the course and eventually joined Bredemus in the course design and construction business. Bredemus moved to Mexico in the late 1930s, but Plummer continued in the golf course design business. He later was chosen by Demaret and Jack Burke Jr. to assist them with the Cypress Creek Course at Champions in 1959. Plummer either designed or did renovation work on the three Texas courses which have hosted the U.S. Open: Colonial in Ft. Worth, Northwood in Dallas, and Champions.

Although during the 1920s almost all of the best golf courses in Houston were private clubs, Jimmy Demaret had the good fortune while he was learning to play golf to have access to two good tests of the game: Memorial Park and River Oaks. At age 16 Demaret started a job at River Oaks Country Club and began working with Jack Burke Sr., who shortly made him caddie master and starter, "with the job of baby-sitting with Jack Burke Jr. thrown in," according to Demaret.

In later years Demaret would joke that he was still baby-sitting Burke Jr., and Burke would retort that the Burke family was still employing Demaret, referring to Demaret working at Champions where they were partners.

Demaret had witnessed the construction of River Oaks, which began in 1922, walking across a foot bridge spanning the bayou along the property. The River Oaks suburb of Houston was developed from 1922 to 1924 by Mike and William Clifford Hogg, and Hugh Potter.

"Donald Ross was the builder, and Jack Burke Sr. came from Ft. Worth as the club's professional," Demaret recalled for *Champions Golf Club: 1957–1976*, by Bob Rule. "I spent so much time over there I soon knew most of the people on the job. That's how I got acquainted with Mr. Burke, and when the club opened he gave me a job as a caddie." Burke made Demaret an assistant pro at the club in 1927.

In the introduction to his instructional series of 45 rpm records, *The Swing's the Thing*, Demaret described his beginnings in the game, when he went to work for Jack Burke Sr. Burke was a golfer of sufficient skill to have finished second in the U.S. Open held at the Inverness Club in Toledo in 1920, losing by one stroke to Edward "Ted" Ray. That Open also featured the first time that clubhouse privileges extended to professional contestants. It was the first Open competition for 18-year-old amateur Bobby Jones, who would win the event in 1923, 1926, 1929, and 1930, and 18-year-old pro Gene Sarazen, who would win it in 1922 and 1932.

"When I had a few minutes, and he [Burke Sr.] did too, he'd help me...help me appreciate the fundamentals of the golf swing," Demaret wrote.

"Those mostly spontaneous get-togethers constitute the whole of my formal education in the proper way to swing a golf club.

I had no lessons before.

I've had none since.

Jack Burke Sr., a man of fundamental conviction about everything in his life, was the same way about the golf swing.

There were things you did when you swung a golf club and there were things you didn't do.

L–R: Ben Hogan, Harold "Jug" McSpaden, Byron Nelson, Jimmy Demaret, and Jack Burke Sr. (courtesy of Brae Burn Country Club)

You did all the fundamental things, and you did nothing else.

First you learned the fundamentals, then you made sure you understood each and its relationship to the other, then you practiced them.

If you lived a hundred years, I was told, nothing you could do, regarding your study of the golf swing, would take you *beyond* the fundamentals."

Demaret's appreciation for this contribution that Jack Burke Sr. made to his playing ability and his career is evident in his dedication for *My Partner, Ben Hogan,* a book that Demaret wrote with Jimmy Breslin in 1954, more than 25 years after Burke's instruction. The dedication reads: "To Jack Burke Sr., who made a professional golfer of me. You can't repay a man for that." In the book Demaret quotes Burke as having told him, "There is a lot more to golf than just hitting a ball—sportsmanship, friends, a whole way of life. You'll find as you go along that you receive as much from the game as you give it."

Burke Sr. was one of the remarkable men in his era who influenced golf throughout the state of Texas during the 18 years he was head professional at River Oaks until his death in 1943. His influence on club pros and competitors who moved to other parts of the nation, and then themselves taught the game, carried forward Burke Sr.'s ideas about golf and extended his legacy. Among these men were Harvey Penick, known for working with Ben Crenshaw and Tom Kite, and Jack Grout, who gave Jack Nicklaus his first lessons when he was 10 years old and worked with him until Grout passed away nearly 40 years later.

A strong competitor himself, Burke Sr. won more than 30 tournaments, mostly at the state level, but as was the case with the 1920 U.S. Open, he finished well in other events. In 1913 he tied for second in the Canadian Open won by Albert Murray at the Royal Montreal Golf Club, the first permanent golf club established on the North American continent, in 1873. His head pro assignments took him from his native Philadelphia to the Midwest and to Port Arthur, Canada, and by 1920 he had managed to win the Minnesota and Kansas State Championships, as well as the 1919 Southwestern title. He won the pro division of the Houston Country Club Invitational in 1920 and the next year finished fourth. He won the Texas PGA Championship five times and the 1941 PGA of America Seniors' Championship. During his visits to Houston for tournaments Burke Sr. had become acquainted with William C. Hunt, who hired Burke to be head pro at River Oaks in 1924.

Donald Ross, the golf course designer of River Oaks, had previously done Galveston Municipal Golf Course, an 18-hole layout now closed, and River Oaks opened as nine holes in 1924, with an additional nine opened in 1927. Ross also has the Sunset Grove Country Club in Orange, Texas attributed to him. At River Oaks he created a golf course that was to host the Western Open in 1940, that event's most southern site in its 100-year history, and a tribute both to the quality of the course and the esteem with which Burke Sr. was held. In Brad Klein's biography of the designer, *Discovering Donald Ross,* he notes that Ross designs have been the sites of 22 U.S. Opens, 16 PGA Championships, 19 U.S. Amateur Championships, and six Ryder

Cups, an event that was also held at Jack Burke Jr.'s creation, Champions Golf Club, in 1967.

Jack Burke Sr.'s ability as a teacher was confirmed by Harvey Penick, author of the *Little Red Book* and other golf books with Bud Shrake, as well as instructor to Tom Kite and Ben Crenshaw during their formative years and beyond. Penick credited Burke with many of the approaches he used in his own teaching.

Jack Burke Jr. described his father's teaching technique: "He taught through stories, and he taught you individually. He used to say that the only system he knew is that there is no system. He taught people as they were. Just like we all come through here with different thumb prints, we can't learn golf at the rate some teachers want to teach it.

"He believed in a great deal of recklessness in the swing. He didn't want you to be so precise. He didn't want you thinking it out so much. Rather, he liked a certain looseness, a certain recklessness in the swing, and he used to teach that."

As proof of how imaginative Burke Sr. was, his son points out that his father perfected the rubber grip that is now commonplace. "He invented the cord-rubber grip that is so popular today," said Jack Jr. "He did that by observing his tire. His tire blew out one day, and he was sitting there looking at that tire while the guy was fixing it, and he saw those cords running through the rubber. It gave him the idea because he thought rubber grips are awfully slippery."

Another Burke Sr. creation was the Blue Goose putter, which he developed with inventor Tracy Parks. The club took its name from the gooseneck shape of the putter head and the blue cast given off by the aluminum alloy used for the club head.

Burke Sr. was a gregarious person who often invited golf pros and people who sold golf products to the Burke home for dinner. "My dad would bring various guys home because he was a curious person, and he always liked to talk and learn," said Jack Jr. "He didn't have much of an education, but he was very educated. He educated himself through dialogue. They liked to listen to him. His stories were like parables. He would teach you through stories, telling what some-one he knew did with reference to what you are trying to do."

Burke Sr. died on February 2, 1943 at age 54. Two weeks later a previously arranged exhibition match to benefit servicemen was go-ing to be held at River Oaks. The match was to feature Byron Nelson, Harold "Jug" McSpaden, Jimmy Demaret, and Burke Sr. The event went on as planned, with Jack Burke Jr., on leave from the Marine Corps for his father's funeral, substituting for his father.

Among the people whose career in golf was influenced by Burke Sr. was Dave Marr, whose father moved his family from Philadelphia to take a position as an assistant pro at River Oaks, and then became pro at Beaumont Country Club. Marr spent some of his childhood years around Burke and later went on to win The PGA Champion-ship in 1965, and had a successful career as a golf analyst on televi-sion.

In Byron Nelson's *The Little Black Book,* Marr recalled how Demaret figured in his family's life: "My father was the golf pro at Beaumont Country Club, and he and Jimmy had double-dated. Dad married mom, and Jimmy married Idella."

When the young Jimmy Demaret began his work at River Oaks Country Club he had the good fortune to work with one of the best instructors in the game, an accomplished competitive golfer, and a man who was one of the most well-acquainted and inventive persons in the entire game of golf. Demaret worked at a quality golf course, one of the best in the entire region. As Burke Sr. would tell him, "You can practice all you want before 6 a.m." It seems that they found a few other occasions to get together on the practice range.

While Demaret credited Burke for sharpening his playing skills, he displayed a remarkable aptitude for the game very early. When Demaret was just 11, he won the Houston city caddie championship by shooting 83 at the Hermann Park course. A little more than two years later he repeated as champion by shooting a 74 when he was 14. He had sufficient organizational skills to be named caddie master when he worked at the Hermann Park course. He later recalled that on rainy days at the course he would hit practice shots off the wooden clubhouse porch, which Robie Williams, a coworker at the time, remembered years later.

Jimmy Demaret's brothers also excelled at golf and spent their careers in the golf business, and competing. Milton Demaret went on to become head pro at Brae Burn Country Club in Houston in 1941, following Jimmy's tenure there from 1936 to 1941. Milton competed in several PGA Tour events during the 1940s. Al Demaret was head pro at Edgewater Club in Chicago and then Ojai Valley in California, eventually working at Bermuda Dunes in Palm Springs, California.

Jimmy would later claim that it was when he became the pro at Galveston's Municipal Course at age 22 that he had sufficient time to really work on his game. Galveston is 40 miles from Houston on the Texas coast, with a steady breeze coming in off the Gulf of Mexico. Byron Nelson remarked in *The Little Black Book*, "Jimmy Demaret was a wonderful wind player."

"Galveston is where I really learned to play in the wind," Demaret recalled. "Because it was so windy we didn't have many golfers until the afternoon when it eased a little, so I was able to practice all morning. I would hit balls into the wind, then practice hitting with a side wind so I could learn to hold the ball into it, then I'd practice downwind to see if I could make the ball hold the greens. I got four years of the greatest experience of my life."

Jack Burke Jr. later recalled Demaret from this time. "I was around 10 or 12 years old, and Jimmy frequently came over from Galveston to play golf with my Dad," said Burke. "They'd always have a few dollars going on their matches because that was the only way a professional could make any money playing the game in those days. There was no tour, and very few professional tournaments of any sort."

While Demaret was still a teenager he left River Oaks and spent two years working with John Bredemus on golf course construction, including working on what became Brae Burn Country Club where Demaret would become head professional in 1936. The course construction experience would be valuable to him later in his career when he developed Champions Golf Club, Onion Creek, and contributed to the design of other layouts. In 1930 at age 20 he returned to Golfcrest as an assistant professional, where he had caddied briefly when he was younger.

Demaret got married to Idella Adams in 1932 and he and his wife had one daughter, Peggy. Mother and daughter later spent time filling several scrapbooks about him.

After going to work in 1932 at the Galveston Municipal Course as head professional, Demaret became friendly with Sam Maceo, who owned the Hollywood Dinner Club there. The club featured live music, including the Glen Gray, George Olson, and Ben Bernie orchestras, and Demaret began joining the bands for occasional vocals. Bernie thought well enough of Demaret's talent to offer him a full-time singing job with his band, and the opportunity appealed to Demaret. Bert Maceo persuaded Demaret to pass on the singing offer by bankrolling more tournament entries for him, joined in the enterprise by Houston oilman D.B. McDonald, a member at Brae Burn Country Club. During 1935 Demaret won $385 by finishing third in the Sacramento Open and $750 for a third-place tie in Agua Caliente, California. Ben Hogan, who Demaret remembered meeting as early as 1932 when Hogan was only 20 years old, was still finishing out of the money at this stage of his career. While Demaret was showing promise by his finishes in professional events, pursuing a career as a tournament golfer was not an option in the 1930s.

In considering Demaret's accomplishments on the PGA Tour, especially when he began his career, it is important to appreciate the conditions for someone pursuing victories in professional events at that time. Demaret won only two PGA Tour events before he was 29 years old, but making a full-time career from earnings from the tour was not feasible in the 1930s. It was not until television brought more money to the game in the late 1950s and the early 1960s that the economics of the tour changed dramatically.

Several factors limited the earning potential of a professional in the 1930s. Purses were limited, and most tournaments only paid money to the top 20 finishers. Byron Nelson later prided himself on finishing in the money in 113 straight events during his prime because

Jimmy Demaret at the piano. (courtesy of The PGA of America)

it revealed how consistently he was playing—he had to play very well to place high enough to earn anything from professional events. Even the Masters when it began did not pay all the finishers in the event.

Holding a full-time club professional's job meant restricted practice time. The club pro gave lessons, ran the shop, and occasionally had the opportunity to play with members at the better private clubs. It was during the winter months, when bad weather shut down the golf courses in the North, that the pros had the opportunity to head to California and Texas for the professional events. It was not until 1934 that the summer months featured an extensive list of events.

Getting to the events was not by private jet, or by air at all. Pros traveled by car over bad roads. There was no interstate highway system in the 1930s. Construction began on that in the mid-1950s.

Poor course conditions were the norm, not the exception. Many professional events were played on municipal layouts that had limited funds for course conditioning. Nelson has said that the greatest change on the PGA Tour from his era to the present was in the enhancement of course conditioning and the development of better golf course turf. In his book, *Byron Nelson: How I Played the Game,* he described the varying course conditions of the early days of the PGA Tour.

"Because local committees were in charge of the tournaments," said Nelson, "there wasn't anyone to oversee course conditions everywhere and make sure fairways, roughs, and greens were the same all across the country.

"Even in one tournament, the committee might have only half of the fairways watered. Or the greens might be watered one day and not the next, or watered on the front half and not the back. Of course, they used different types of grasses, too. Common Bermuda in the South and Southwest, and rye, *poa annua,* bluegrass, or bent in the North and East. They used a particular type of German bent at Oakmont, Inverness, and Merion that I never saw anywhere else. Each type of grass behaved differently. Some had more grain, some were slower, some grew faster—all of which made a big difference, depending on what time of day you played."

Besides playing in the event, pros were frequently called upon to promote attendance at the tournaments by making appearances at business clubs or other functions in the host city. Many events were preceded by a parade, a long-driving competition, or other entertainment.

Most importantly, the 1930s were a period of economic depression, a condition that was not alleviated significantly until World War II. Then rationing became necessary, including a ban on the manufacture of golf equipment and golf balls because the materials were needed in the war effort.

Chandler Harper, who went on to win The PGA Championship in 1950, described his early days on tour in Al Barkow's book *Gettin' to the Dance Floor.* "What we were trying to do was make a reputation so we could make money some other way. Nobody had any idea of making any on the tour," said Harper. "We were all trying to do something that would put us in a position to get a good club job and make a good living."

Harper had turned professional in 1934 after a successful career in amateur competitions in his home state of Virginia. In one of his first PGA Tour appearances in Indianapolis, Harper played well enough to earn a check for $130. Before leaving town, he used the check to pay his hotel bill, receiving some change back. He went on to Louisville for his next event when he received word that the checks issued in Indianapolis were no good. Since the hotel never contacted him, Harper assumed the event account had enough to cover his check.

His first job as an assistant pro was at Truxton Manor Public Course in Norfolk, Virginia in 1934. In his book *My First Seventy Years in Golf,* Harper recalled that on weekdays the course would have less than ten golfers come through each day. In 1938 when Harper played in the Los Angeles Open his entire hotel bill for the week was $12. That week he ate at a restaurant in Hollywood where a dinner with shrimp cocktail, main course, and dessert cost "exactly one dollar."

Harper also recalled Clayton Heafner in the late 1930s announcing to him that he was quitting the PGA Tour, which was during a year that Heafner was leading in the race for the Vardon Trophy. "This is a rat race," Heafner told Harper. "There's no money out here. I've had enough of this." Heafner built a golf course that he operated in Charlotte, North Carolina, but continued on the PGA Tour. This was the man about whom Demaret would comment, "He's the most even-tempered player on Tour—he's mad all the time." Before he became a regular on the PGA Tour Heafner had worked in a North Carolina confectionery factory. Demaret described Heafner as "an ex-candy mechanic—he used to screw the nuts in the peanut brittle."

In his book *The History of the PGA Tour,* Barkow described those early circumstances for the professional: "The fact was that for every Leo Diegel who had a cushy deal in California that gave him all the time he wanted to play tournaments, there were 10 men the likes of Horton Smith, winner of the first and third Masters tournaments, who held club jobs in the summer with contracts stating specifically how many—or how few—tournaments they could play in."

The first professional victory for Demaret was the 1934 Texas PGA at Dallas. He could not afford to pay a caddie that the event would provide, so Demaret promised to split his winnings with Charley Schwartz, a Houston caddie, if he would come to Dallas with him. They hopped a freight train for transportation, "our complete baggage consisting of two clean shirts and a single toothbrush," as he recalled the trip in *My Partner, Ben Hogan.* He earned $25 for the win, which allowed the two to ride a passenger train back to Houston, although Demaret admitted that it took him two years before he paid the room tab where he and Charley had stayed at the Hotel Waco in Dallas. Demaret would go on to win the Texas PGA the next three years, an event that his mentor Jack Burke Sr. had previously won, then Demaret won it again in 1945.

The year Demaret won his first professional event, 1934, was pivotal in golf. The first Augusta National Invitational, which would in coming years become known as the Masters, was played March 22–25. Paul Runyan was the first official leading money winner on tour with $6,767 in 1934, winning seven events to accomplish those earnings. An indication of how much the tour struggled during the 1930s is the fact that total purses had declined from $130,000 in 1935 to $117,000 by 1940, with Ben Hogan capturing his first earnings title that year with $10,655.

Bob Harlow, hired in 1930 as manager of the PGA Tournament Bureau, later to become the PGA Tour, raised the total purse money on tour from $70,000 to its $130,000 level by 1935. Harlow first proposed the idea of expanding "The Circuit," as the Tour was known in 1930, from a series of winter events leading up to the season-ending North & South Open in spring, into a year-round Tour. Part of what transformed the financial rewards for the golf professionals was corporate sponsorship of events, which began in 1933 with the Hershey Chocolate Company sponsoring the Hershey Open in Pennsylvania. Fred Corcoran became the manager of the PGA Tour in late 1936

Fred Corcoran, manager of the PGA Tour, and Demaret. (courtesy of The PGA of America)

and his promotional skills helped create more opportunities for the pros.

Another indication of the financial circumstances for professional golfers in the 1930s is the fact that the biggest payday for a professional golfer that decade came in 1930 when Bobby Cruickshank made $60,000 on a bet that Bobby Jones would win the Grand Slam (U.S. Open, U.S. Amateur, British Open, and British Amateur). Cruickshank had placed his bet when the odds stood at 120:1.

Even the Masters in its early days featured a calcutta, a betting pool where the participants were able to place bets on themselves or their fellow competitors. David Owen in his book *The Making of the Masters* describes the gambling action of that era.

"Beginning in 1934, the club had participated indirectly in the operation of a public Masters auction pool, or calcutta," wrote Owen, "a standard feature at golf tournaments in that era—which was held at the Bon Air Hotel; there were numerous other pools as well, including some at the club itself. (The last Masters calcutta conducted at Augusta National was held in 1952.)"

The decade of the 1930s was also a time when golf marathons were held, with golfers trying to play as many holes as possible in the shortest amount of time. Miniature golf courses were popular and even water golf was being played, with golfers being rowed around on small dinghies, hitting floating golf balls to floating golf holes.

Demaret became head professional at Brae Burn Country Club in February 1936, and he remained there until March 1941. The announcement of his new position was carried in the *Houston Post* sports section, along with a photo of Demaret.

"Demaret, a product of Houston municipal courses, is 25 years of age and ranks as one of the finest shotmakers in the Southwest," the article said. "He picked up the art of shotmaking at the old Camp Logan and Hermann Park courses.

"A natural golfer, Jimmy developed fast and at the age of 20 was rated as one of the most promising young players in the country. He worked as assistant at Hermann Park for some time and then was

Brae Burn Country Club in the 1940s. (courtesy of Brae Burn Country Club)

named as assistant to Jack Burke, pro at River Oaks Country Club course."

Ray Ayles got a job at Brae Burn toward the end of Demaret's tenure there and stayed with the club for the rest of his career. In 2003, after more than 60 years at Brae Burn, he remembered how Demaret returned to Houston one year after the Masters, disgusted with himself for taking a five putt during one round. Always capable of laughing at himself, Demaret bought a Chris-Craft 23-foot boat and named it Mr. Five Putt. Demaret and Bob Hope attended the festivities when Brae Burn christened its new clubhouse in the 1960s.

In his first golf season at Brae Burn in 1936, Demaret was host pro when the club held the Texas Cup matches. The event featured teams of amateurs and professionals from across the state competing. The amateur team had players of national significance, including Ed White, national intercollegiate champion of 1935 and a member of the Walker Cup team, and Reynolds Smith, another Walker Cup team member. Joining Demaret on the professionals' team was Harvey Penick from Austin.

Another indication of how golf professionals viewed their opportunities on tour in the 1930s was the arrangement made in 1935 between Demaret and Jack Grout when they traveled together. They decided to pool their traveling money and then split their winnings, which didn't result in any gain for either of them.

Demaret's early performance on the PGA Tour was not remarkable. In 1935, he had two top 10 finishes and three top 25 on the PGA Tour. Playing in his first PGA Championship that year, he was eliminated in his first round match. Jack Burke Sr. had missed qualifying for the tournament by shooting 156 in the 36-hole qualifier.

In 1936 Demaret had one top 10 and five top 25 finishes, and again he was eliminated in his first round match in The PGA Championship. He didn't fare as well in 1937, and had one top 10 and two top 25, including finishing in a tie for 16th in the U.S. Open held at Oakland Hills in Detroit. Once again, he lost his first round match in The PGA Championship. To compare how he improved over the years, he had 15 or more top 10 finishes every year from 1946 through 1950, peaking with 23 top 10 finishes in 1947, the year he finished first on the money list and won the Vardon Trophy for low scoring average.

One nontournament round played by Demaret in 1937, witnessed by Harvey Penick in Austin on August 2, is worth noting. Visiting Austin Country Club where Penick was employed, and working on a theory that the elbows should stay together through the swing, Demaret shot 28 on the front nine, and 32 on the back for a 60. His card showed four straight 3s for the first four holes, 10 birdies total, and no bogeys for the entire round. The scorecard is shown in an article Penick did for the April 1960 issue of *Golf Digest*.

In Harvey Penick's book *And If You Play Golf, You're My Friend*, written with Bud Shrake and published over 30 years later, Penick describes the round again, but this time he has Demaret shooting a 59.

Demaret in his early days on the PGA Tour. (courtesy of Charles Newman)

"What is it you are trying to do with your swing?" Penick asked him on the tee.

"I am trying to keep my elbows out in front of me on my follow-through."

Penick then watched Demaret shoot 30-29 — 59. Ever since that time, Penick said, "keeping the elbows out in front on the follow-through has been one of the things I emphasize in teaching."

It was Demaret's versatility as a shotmaker that Penick attributed as the reason for his success as a competitor.

"Jimmy Demaret could hit more different shots than anyone else who ever won major championships on the tour," said Penick. "Only a great trick-shot artist like Joe Kirkwood could hit as many different shots as Jimmy—low, high, hook, slice, whatever he wanted.

"Jimmy had the forearms of a giant and could hit that little ball in what he called a 'quail shot' that didn't go more than two or three feet off the ground."

Penick liked Demaret's follow-through on his swing so much that he taped a photograph of Demaret's finish to his office window.

Demaret finally had his breakthrough year in 1938, finishing in the top 10 six times and the same number for top 25, but more importantly, he won his first PGA Tour event in February of 1938, in the San Francisco match play event. He missed the cut at the U.S. Open at Cherry Hills in Denver, but he finally advanced past the first round in The PGA Championship, winning two matches before losing to Gene Sarazen in the third round.

His victory in San Francisco earned him a headline in the *New York Times* sports section of February 14, 1938—"Demaret Defeats Snead by 4 and 3." His reputation for being able to handle bad weather conditions began with this event. "The Texan—he was born, reared, and learned golf in Houston—produced a consistent and remarkable game in the face of the worst weather that ever prevailed for a major tournament in this part of the country," the story said, the term "major" at that time not restricted to only the four most important events on the tour. Major event usually meant a PGA Tour event as opposed to a tournament with only local, state, or regional competitors.

"Snead consistently outhit Demaret by 30 to 40 yards, but off-line shots and erratic putting combined to offset this advantage," said the article in the *New York Times*. "Demaret was consistent if not particularly brilliant to haul down $1,000 top money." The newspaper story described the match as "fought in rain, wind, and spongy turf."

Demaret's next PGA Tour win was the Los Angeles Open in January of 1939. His loose and comfortable manner appealed to many golf fans in Hollywood and he became friends with several people in the movie community. The victory in the Los Angeles Open was by a commanding seven strokes over second-place finisher Harold "Jug" McSpaden. Demaret shot rounds of 66, 68, 71, and 69, missing the tournament record by one shot. A highlight of Demaret's final round came at the par-5 eighth hole where he sank a 21-foot putt for an eagle. McSpaden, playing in the group ahead of Demaret in the final round, and with the tournament out of reach, on the 18th hole called his approach shot from the fairway some 180 yards out and holed the shot, eliciting a roar from the crowd surrounding the green. A total of 245 amateurs and professionals qualified for the event.

A week after his victory in Los Angeles Demaret was competing in the Houston Open, a 54-hole event. He finished fourth, five strokes behind the winner, McSpaden. Hogan finished three strokes ahead of Demaret, and Byron Nelson finished two behind Jimmy.

During 1939 Demaret served as the golf coach for the Rice University team, but he was allowed to work with the players for only one day a week. The team won the Southwest Conference Championship that year. The captain of the golf team was Joe Finger, who went on to become a golf course architect, with the Championship Course, also known as the Monster, at the Concord Hotel in New York being one of his designs.

On Labor Day weekend of 1939 another golf course design by John Bredemus opened in Corpus Christi, Texas. Jimmy Demaret participated in the opening festivities, along with Sam Schneider, Jack Burke Sr., and Edwin "Beetle" Juelg, who was named as the first professional. Milton Demaret, Jimmy's brother, was named the assistant professional.

With the strong win in Los Angeles, one of the premier events on tour, Demaret had shown what he could accomplish. He ended the year with five top 25 finishes, four of them among the top 10. Demaret in 1939 finished tied for 33rd in his first Masters, tied for 22nd in the U.S. Open, and he did not enter The PGA Championship. Though he was 29 years old by the end of the year, he had another 18 productive years ahead of him as a PGA Tour player, and for the rest of his life he would be one of the most prominent people in the entire golf business.

CHAPTER 2

A DECADE BORDERED IN GREEN

"An Easygoing, Eye-pleasing Fellow"

◆ ◆ ◆

Demaret established himself as among the best players on tour early in 1940, dominating the first four months of the golf season. This was the year when his potential was realized, when he won five events (three in a row) during the winter tour before he even reached the Masters in early April. He had won in Oakland, San Francisco, Houston (the Western Open at River Oaks on February 21, the only professional event he was to win in his hometown), New Orleans, and St. Petersburg.

At the same time that Demaret began to receive serious attention on the national scene, Jack Burke Jr., eldest son of Jack Burke Sr., turned pro on January 6, 1940, beginning a career that included 17 wins on the PGA Tour, a series of four victories in a row during the 1952 season, and Masters and PGA Championship victories in 1956. Jack Jr.'s father had taken Jimmy with him to tournaments to show off the newcomer, and Demaret would repeat the favor as Jack Jr. was developing as a player. It was on one such trip to the West Coast that Bob Hope met the young Jack Burke Jr. and learned that he was a golf professional. "Where? Boys Town?" was Hope's rejoinder.

In winning the Western Open at River Oaks in February 1940, Demaret had to defeat his MacGregor Golf Clubs colleague Tony

Elroy Marti, a touring professional from Houston, Demaret, Hogan, seated, and Nelson at Brae Burn Country Club. (courtesy of Brae Burn Country Club)

Penna in a play-off. After falling behind by two shots by the fourth hole, Demaret birdied three of the next four holes in completing the front nine. A seven-foot putt on the 18th hole gave Demaret his fifth birdie for the day and a round of one under to Penna's three over par.

Jimmy's younger brother Mahlon, age 17, caddied for him during the Western Open. Asked if he caddied for Jimmy very much, Mahlon replied jokingly, "No, not often. He didn't pay very much. I wanted to caddie for a guy who had some money."

Mahlon's wife Mercedes recalled that Jimmy owned a golf driving range on South Main in Houston in the early 1940s. Mahlon worked there for several years. "I was out there when Jimmy's wife told me we were at war," said Mahlon. "That was December the 7th, 1941."

Known for being as relaxed a golfer who ever set foot on a links anywhere, Demaret's participation in the "Music Match" in 1940 in

Norwalk, Connecticut illustrates how comfortable he could be even while enduring substantial distractions. Fred Corcoran, then the PGA Tour's promotion wizard, organized a golf event featuring Demaret, Gene Sarazen, Gene Tunney, and Jack Dempsey (the last two gentlemen being noted boxers of the era), who would compete while Fred Waring's big-band orchestra would be playing on the course. The event attracted a crowd of 5,000 curious spectators interested in witnessing and hearing the spectacle. Despite the cacophony, Demaret shot 70 and Sarazen a 71. It may be that this exhibition was part of the inspiration for Demaret's later production of a golf instruction series accompanied by music called *The Swing's the Thing.*

Demaret's attire soon became a regular element of golf writers' coverage of his participation in golf events. Reporting for the *New York Times* in 1940, William Richardson wrote: "One of the most picturesque figures the game has ever produced, an easygoing, eye-pleasing fellow who really seems to be enjoying himself in tournament play, Demaret went out today (the final round) as though he were starting out to play a round with no more depending on it than a $5 or $10 nassau, garbed in his usual green ensemble with the brim of his hat turned up in front and down in back to give him a rakish appearance."

In Tom Flaherty's book *The Masters,* he describes Demaret's fabled nonchalance while enduring the pressure of tournament play. "On the final green at St. Petersburg Byron Nelson had canned a birdie putt and left Demaret needing a four-footer to win. While the gallery tensed, Demaret sauntered up to his ball, smiled at it in mock tenderness, looked up at the crowd, and chirped, 'Would anyone like to sink this one for me?' While the gallery chuckled, Jimmy sank his own putt."

Ben Hogan won his first PGA Tour event in 1940, and went on to win the next two weeks. By the time 17 events had been played on tour that year, Demaret, winning six, and Hogan, winning four, accounted for ten of the victories. Despite being one of the hottest players on tour for the first six months of the year, at the U.S. Open in June Demaret didn't get off to a good start. Despite being among

Demaret during the 1940 San Francisco Match Play Championship. (courtesy of Associated Press)

the favorites to win the event, he opened with an 81 and did not even turn in his scorecard.

On March 11, 1941 an article ran in the *Houston Post* announcing that Demaret would be moving to the Wee Burn Club in Noroton, Connecticut near New York City, assuming his new duties on April 15. The club was founded in 1896.

"I hate to leave Houston, but the offer in Connecticut was too attractive," Demaret was quoted as saying at the time. "This city has been kind to me, the Brae Burn Club has been wonderful, and it's tough leaving."

The article noted that Demaret would have more time to pursue playing on the tour since he would not be in residency at Wee Burn for more than six months out of the year. Having sufficient time to practice his game and enter tournaments was becoming important to him. "Al Demaret, assistant pro at the country club here, and Jimmy's brother, has kept a record of his winter score," the article said, "and discovered that Jimmy was 25 strokes better than he was at this time last year, but instead of winning six championships, he hasn't gathered a single one." During his tenure at Wee Burn, Demaret added the Connecticut Open to his list of titles. His friend and mentor Jack Burke Sr. won the PGA Seniors' Championship in 1941, his first national title.

Tom Flaherty in his book *The Masters* described how the opportunity at Wee Burn helped Demaret to hone his skills. "For six weeks he played 27 holes a day, in a campaign to perfect his putting on the Eastern greens. The tonic worked, and before long the Demaret golf game was again in a class with the Demaret personality."

The first victory in four-ball competition for the team of Ben Hogan and Jimmy Demaret was the Inverness Four-Ball in June of 1941 at Inverness Country Club in Toledo, Ohio. The club has been the site of four U.S. Opens and a PGA Championship.

Hogan partnered with Demaret to win six official four-ball events on the PGA Tour during the 1940s and early 1950s, and they also played together in Ryder Cup competition. On many occasions

Demaret and Hogan hold the Inverness Cup, which they won as a team four times. (courtesy of The PGA of America)

throughout their careers they competed head-to-head against each other. Hogan's drubbing of Demaret 10 and 9 in the semifinal of the 1946 PGA Championship, a 36-hole match format that ended after 27 holes, was one notable contest, and Demaret finishing 5 strokes ahead of Hogan in the 1950 Masters is another. They had finished 1-2 alternately in the two PGA Tour events leading up to Hogan's car accident in 1949. Hogan beat Demaret in a play-off for the Long

Ben Hogan, left foreground, instructs, while Demaret, with microphone on the right, narrates during a playing clinic. (courtesy of The PGA of America)

Beach Open title on January 24, then the following week on January 30, Demaret beat Hogan in a play-off for the Phoenix Open. Two days later Hogan had the car accident that nearly ended his career.

In the early days of the PGA Tour a four-ball tournament was popular with host clubs because it meant a reduced field of players. The requirements to operate the event were less than with a full field event, and that meant lower expenses, fewer volunteers necessary, and a more manageable program all around. The participants in most PGA Tour events from the 1920s into the 1950s were rarely a full field of professionals. Local club pros and amateurs were solicited to participate and provide a large enough field to make the events more appealing to spectators. As purses rose in the 1950s and events featured all professionals, the four-ball format became untenable, though it still survives as a popular amateur competition and as part of the Ryder Cup Matches.

When he wrote *My Partner, Ben Hogan,* Demaret described the attributes that made Hogan so competitive: "Ben's hot rounds come from five different sources besides just his superior ability with golf clubs; these are not clear-cut separate assets, but in combination they are all but impossible to beat. In order of their importance they are: (1) his intense determination to win; (2) a temperamental makeup, which just doesn't have a letting-up point—the match is never over for Ben; (3) his complete concentration; (4) his quiet confidence in his ability to shellack you nine and eight; (5) more practice than any other golfer has ever taken. Add these intangibles all together and they spell out probably the finest competitive golfer ever to step onto a tee."

A tour of several South American countries for Demaret and Sam Snead was announced in August of 1941, with their departure scheduled for late September and return in time to play in the Miami Open in December. Exhibition matches between the two were scheduled for Panama, São Paulo and Rio de Janeiro, Brazil, and Puerto Rico. Showing that his game traveled well, Demaret won the Argentine Open on the trip. His score of 279 was the lowest recorded in the 37-year history of the event through that time.

Within a year of moving to Wee Burn, Demaret moved again, this time to Plum Hollow in the Detroit area. One of the highlights of his tenure there was a match on May 2, 1942 between a team of Bob Hope/Walter Hagen and Demaret/Detroit Mayor Ed Jeffries, won by the Demaret/Jeffries team 2-up. On September 7, a match between Bing Crosby/Demaret and a team of Byron Nelson/Chick Harbert, who won 4 and 3, drew a crowd of 5,000 spectators. After making a birdie four on the 18th hole, Crosby sang "Home on the Range" from the middle of the green.

During World War II Demaret definitely lost what should have been nearly three productive years on tour, at a critical time in his playing career. He was 31 when the war began in December 1941 and he turned 35 in May of 1945. He wasn't past his prime at that point, as

the inside story of professional golf and its greatest player

My Partner, BEN HOGAN *by* Jimmy Demaret

Cover of the book, My Partner, Ben Hogan, *published in 1954 by McGraw-Hill.*

he had his best year on tour in 1947, and he continued to win on the PGA Tour through 1957, but given the level of his play he might have added eight to ten more wins during these years.

He played in about 50 USO golf exhibitions during 1942 and still competed in professional events. He finished sixth in the Masters, won by Byron Nelson, and Demaret tied for fourth at the Land of the Sky Open in Asheville, NC, which was won by Ben Hogan. At the Western Open in Phoenix he finished tied for 21st, winning the

Ticket to a World War II relief golf exhibition at Brae Burn Country Club. *(courtesy of Brae Burn Country Club)*

Autographs of Crosby, Nelson, Hope, and Demaret on the ticket back. *(courtesy of Brae Burn Country Club)*

grand sum of $41.66, not unusual for the era. At the Inverness Four-Ball he and partner Ben Hogan finished tied for fourth, one of the few times they did not win as a team. In August his score of 285 at the

Rochester Open in New York left him seven strokes behind his friend Hogan, the winner.

The USGA, the Chicago District Golf Association, and The PGA of America in July 1942 staged the Hale America National Open, a fund-raiser for Navy Relief and the USO. The title of the event referred to a campaign to keep America's war-workers fit and productive. Hogan won the event and ever after claimed the victory as another U.S. Open crown, although that has never been officially recognized. Demaret finished second, four strokes back, along with Mike Turnesa.

Moraine Country Club in Dayton, Ohio, was the site of one of the exhibitions Demaret played in during 1942. Colonel E.A. Deeds, the founder of the club, spoke at the dinner following the exhibition.

"Today, I saw a fine thing happen....Through the years, we have spent much time and money in building and maintaining Moraine's fairways," said Deeds. "But not until today have I seen these fairways in use. Apparently, our members prefer the tall, uncut grass, and gentleman I thank you for your fine demonstrations today of just what fairways are really for."

The PGA Tour was essentially shut down during 1943. The imposition of gas rationing limited travel to courses, and new golf balls were banned from being manufactured. Because of the limited access to rubber, which was important for use in the war effort, the chemical industry began exploring new synthetic covers for golf balls. The development and manufacturing of more durable golf balls certainly benefited the average golfer.

Demaret did participate in a few events during 1943. He won the Michigan PGA Championship that year. In September he paired with Craig Wood to win the Golden Valley four-ball tournament. In August at the Chicago Victory Open he finished eight strokes behind victor Sam Byrd, who succeeded Demaret as head professional at Plum Hollow. A month earlier he had competed in the All American Open in Chicago and he finished tied for eleventh.

On November 8, 1943 it was announced that Demaret would become the head professional at River Oaks Country Club, succeeding

*Johnny Weissmuller, star of the Tarzan movies in the 1930s, Bob Hope,
Demaret, Byron Nelson, and Bing Crosby at Brae Burn Country Club. (courtesy
of Brae Burn Country Club)*

his former mentor Jack Burke Sr., who had died on February 2, 1943.
Returning to Houston was a welcome opportunity for Demaret.
River Oaks was where he had learned much of what he knew about
the game of golf from Jack Burke Sr., but Burke's passing at age 54
had to have made the River Oaks opportunity bittersweet.

He would have less than two weeks to work at River Oaks in 1943.
Entering the U.S. Navy within two weeks of returning to work at the
club, Demaret would not return on a regular basis to competition on
tour events until 1945, and he did not assess his own game as back to
form until 1946. Claude Harmon replaced Demaret as the head professional at the club during the time Demaret was in the service.

With the end of the war in sight by 1944, 22 PGA Tour tournaments were staged, with total purses of $150,000, a considerable gain from the total in 1940, but the professionals received war bonds as compensation, whose value at the time of issue was 75% of the face value. Jimmy's brother Milton played in the New Orleans Open in late February, finishing 17th, and the following year he would place T-17th at the Gulfport Open in Gulfport, Mississippi. Jimmy obtained leave from the Navy in early June of 1944 to participate in the Philadelphia Inquirer event, placing 22nd.

During 1945, a year when Byron Nelson owned the PGA Tour with 18 official victories, and one more in an event that didn't have a sufficient total purse to be considered an official tour victory, Demaret played in two of the events that were part of Nelson's streak of 11 straight tour wins, a record still not equaled nor surpassed. Demaret had six top 25 finishes for the year.

Nelson did not back into his victories; his scoring average for 38 rounds was 67.92. He simply played better than everyone else. Nelson's remarkable play brought a level of attention to the PGA Tour that it had never known. Even nongolfers could understand that winning all the time is rare in any sport. As the streak continued it became as important as Joe DiMaggio's streak of hitting safely in 56 straight games during the 1941 baseball season. That new level of recognition for the tour helped grow spectator interest when the war ended and the tour resumed its full schedule. All professional golfers were helped by the publicity generated by Nelson's achievements. He was named the Associated Press Male Athlete of the Year for 1944 and 1945.

One of the highlights of 1945 came in a three-week period from September 27 through October 14. First, Hogan shot rounds of 65-69-63-64—261 to win the Portland Invitational by 14 strokes. Nelson finished 14 strokes behind him in second place. At the Seattle Open three weeks later, Nelson shot 62-68-63-66—259 in winning that event by 13 shots, with Hogan 20 strokes behind him in ninth place.

When considering Demaret's accomplishments as a professional golfer it is important to appreciate the level of his competition, among them Nelson, Hogan, and Snead, who between them accounted for 196 PGA Tour victories during their careers. When the PGA World Golf Hall of Fame had its first inductions in 1974, all three players were inducted. The Vardon Trophy for the PGA Tour season's best scoring average was awarded to Snead in 1938, Nelson in 1939, Hogan in 1940 and 1941, and suspended from 1942 through 1946 for World War II. Then Demaret won it in 1947, followed by Hogan in '48 and Snead in '49, '50, and '55. Two other players active during Demaret's career, Lloyd Mangrum and Cary Middlecoff, accounted for a total of 76 PGA Tour victories, putting them among the top 12 in number of victories, and between them having four victories in majors. Despite having some of the best players ever to play on Tour for competition, Demaret managed 31 victories himself.

Al Barkow had the opportunity to witness Demaret as a player on tour and to know him as a colleague during the time they worked together on *Shell's Wonderful World of Golf.* In his book, *Golf's Golden Grind, A History of the PGA Tour,* Barkow gives a description of Demaret on the golf course during his playing days. "In preparing to play a shot, Demaret pranced up to the ball from behind it, his head tilted like someone lining up a billiard shot, his body slightly angled to the left of his line, and the club spinning constantly in his hands. Once over the ball, Demaret kept his feet quite close together and lined them up generally well left of the target. Just before taking the club back he would shove it along the ground until the ball was in the very neck, or shank, of the club. As soon as the club got into that position he took it up. He would cut across the ball from outside to inside his line of flight, and the ball would invariably fly from left to right."

Just after the end of World War II, the Cavalier Country Club in Virginia hosted the Specialists Tournament, which featured a format of two eight-man teams, with a different team member to play each of the various shots. Jimmy Demaret captained one team and Chandler Harper captained the other one. Harper remembered the event in his book *My First Seventy Years in Golf.* "Lew Worsham was on Demaret's team. He and Jimmy were close friends. On the fifth hole,

Worsham topped his tee shot into a sand trap. The gallery gasped at seeing a player of his caliber hit such a shot. Demaret said to the gallery, 'Ladies and gentlemen, what do you expect of this man? He wears a six shoe and fifteen hat!'"

In February of 1946 Demaret resigned his position as head professional at River Oaks. In his next position Demaret's club affiliation changed from being a head professional to being a touring pro. Head professionals had management responsibilities in their jobs that frequently prevented them from participating in professional tournaments, or certainly traveling for extended periods of time. A touring pro was primarily a representative of a club, bringing recognition to the club, playing with club members occasionally, and even attracting other noted professionals and celebrities to visit the club.

Demaret's first touring pro affiliation was with Ojai Valley Inn in California. Built by wealthy Ohio glass manufacturer Edward Drummond Libbey, the Ojai (pronounced oh-hi) Valley Inn & Spa opened as a 206-room resort in 1923. Located 73 miles northwest of Los Angeles, the property's setting is a pastoral valley surrounded by the Topa Topa Mountains. The par-70 golf course was designed by George C. Thomas Jr. and Billy Bell. Thomas is also known for his work on the golf courses at the Riviera, Bel-Air, and Los Angeles country clubs.

After World War II, Don B. Burger renovated the Inn, with contributions from investors that included actresses Irene Dunne and Loretta Young, and actor Randolph Scott. Demaret himself ultimately became an investor. Fresh from his 1947 Masters victory, Demaret was named the Ojai's touring professional. Jimmy's brother Al would later work as head professional at the resort. Ben Hogan and George Fazio participated in an exhibition match at the resort, which was visited on a regular basis by the stars of Hollywood. Jack Benny, Bing Crosby, Bob Hope, Clark Gable, Rita Hayworth, Anthony Quinn, and Lana Turner were among the resort guests into the 1950s. The MGM film *Pat and Mike,* made in 1952 and based on the life of Babe Didrickson Zaharias, starred Katherine Hepburn and Spencer Tracy. The film included golf scenes shot on the resort's no.

1 and 7 holes. Earlier the property was the setting for the 1937 film *Lost Horizons,* directed by Frank Capra.

Despite his layoff from golf during the war, Demaret returned to winning form promptly. He was fourth on the money winner list for 1946, and he would finish in the top 10 in golf earnings every year from 1946 through 1950. He had three wins, three seconds, and five third-place finishes during 1946. His 25 top 25 finishes reflected how consistently he was playing and that he was back to his best form.

The earnings list was led by Ben Hogan in 1946, who won 13 tournaments, the second highest number of victories in a single year on tour, followed by Herman Barron in second, and Byron Nelson, who had retired late that summer, in third. Demaret won the Tucson Open and teamed with Hogan to win the Miami and Inverness Four-Ball events. Demaret finished tied for second at the Philadelphia Inquirer Tournament one week prior to the U.S. Open in June.

Demaret in 1946 revisited Oso Beach Golf and Country Club in Corpus Christi, where he had participated in course opening festivities in 1939. The course became a municipal layout in 1946 and the Corpus Christi Golf Association organized a "World Championship Four-Ball Match" to promote the golf club. The match featured four of the best players of the era: Jimmy Demaret, Ben Hogan, Byron Nelson, and Sam Snead.

At The PGA Championship at Portland Golf Club in Oregon, Demaret's close personal friend Ben Hogan managed to thump him 10 & 9 in the semifinals, one of the four times Demaret advanced that far in the event. When Hogan beat Porky Oliver in the final it would be his first major championship victory. Hogan seemed determined to make up for time lost during the war years, winning 13 events during 1946. Another indication of how golf was garnering more interest was the forming of what became the Golf Writers Association of America during the playing of The PGA Championship. The year ended with the announcement of Byron Nelson's retirement from regular tour participation.

Demaret began 1947 on a tear, and he went on to end the year as top money winner on tour and capture the Vardon Trophy, which

Demaret found the galleries at the golf tournaments as appealing as they viewed him. He explained his attitude toward the spectators in an article in *Professional Golfer*, the magazine of The PGA of America, which was distributed to the club professionals across America—it was not directed to an audience of average golfers. As the tour made its way around the country many local pros, and amateurs for that matter, would participate in PGA Tour events to fill out the field. The pros who did travel with the tour also had club affiliations. The article shows that Demaret understood professional golfers to have a responsibility to promote the game and engage the spectators' interest. The article was titled "We're All 'Gallery Bit'."

"To me, the faces of spectators in a golf gallery are the most interesting in the world. They express the inward feelings of the player himself. Chagrin or joy can be registered in a moment ... all depending on how the shot goes. The most ardent followers of some of the stars actually seem to suffer far more than the player when things go wrong. They're wonderful folks, these tournament spectators!

Wanta know one reason why I wear those 'noisy' togs along toward the finals of a tournament? (That is, if I get toward the finals.)

I'm 'gallery bit.' In fact, most of the touring boys are, in advanced stages.

'Gallery-bite' gives you a burning desire to entertain the gallery, and, incidentally, give them something that may help their own game.

I don't mean that the sleek, well-groomed Ben Hogan, or the sartorial Craig Wood let their tournament toggery go hogwild just because they're 'gallery-bitten,' but I do mean that we who have been so fortunate as to rise to the top ranks in our playing profession feel an obligation to the galleries who pay their money to see us in action. And if, in my case, the folks like to see my yellow and orange haberdashery bobbing along the fairways (and the rough), who am I to say no? (Besides, I like to wear 'loud' golf toggery.)

More seriously, I believe that we owe it to the paying folks to give them the brand of golf they like, and to remember at all times that the only reason they crowd around and let go with some yells now and then is because they are getting a thrill.

Far be it from me to prescribe that the pros who are in it to win the folding money should deliberately seek out the roughs and the unplayable lies, but when we do get that way, we must remember that the folks standing around—not hoping we'll fail to get out, but wanting to know *how* we get out.

I believe that every pro has the obligation at all times of playing his best, even though he feels he is out of the running. And don't you forget that human nature is funny, and that sometimes it's the pulse of the crowd that can lift us out of trouble and put us back into the running.

Out of the corner of my eye, I watch the galleries, and I love 'em. They're nice people. They study the game seriously, and they have a sense of humor. But woe betide the pro who loses his own sense of humor when the going's tough and the fairway is lined with the folks who came to watch us.

For my part, it's something like being on the stage. Players before an empty house lack a very vital response, and it is the same on the tournament golf course. When you can feel the tension of five or ten thousand people hanging on what happens to that putt, when you can hear the silence crackle as you try to get out from behind that tree—when you've got to play a ball out of someone's heelmark—then is when your real playing pro rises to heights. And—peculiarly enough—I am not so sure that it's entirely due to the bag of gold at the 19th hole. I like to think that part of this eternal thrill is in just knowing that the folks are close by—crowding against the rope perhaps—but close by, holding their breath and hoping we make the shot a good one.

I believe that golf galleries want every golfer's shot to count, rather than to hope someone's shot will go wrong. They don't want any golfer to lose—they'd like to have everyone win! The greatest thrill in golf, for the galleries, is to see a man get into trouble—and get out of it.

'Gallery-bit'? ... I sure am! And if I'm ever cured, golf's not going to be nearly so much fun—nor so lucrative."

starting that year was based on stroke average instead of a point system. By March 10 that year he had captured two victories, setting a tournament record in winning his second straight Tucson Open, with a total of 264. He also placed second in two events, then partnered with Ben Hogan to win the International four-ball championship in Miami. He won his second Masters in April and one week later shot a 66 in the final round of the North Fulton Open in Atlanta to win that event.

Bob Hope had Demaret on his popular radio show on January 28, 1947, along with Ben Hogan. Hope's affinity for golf lasted throughout his career and he frequently had successful golfers as guests on his radio show. In May of 1942 and November of 1944 Bobby Jones was a guest; in January of 1946 Byron Nelson was a guest; and Demaret also came on the show in January of 1951 and January of 1952, both of these later appearances being joined by Bing Crosby. Demaret described Hope's golf in the statement, "Bob Hope has a wonderful short game. Unfortunately, it's off the tee."

Sportswriter Grantland Rice, whose column was syndicated nationally by the North American Newspaper Alliance, and who had witnessed many of the achievements of Bobby Jones during the 1920s, was inspired to poetry by Demaret's feats, but maybe more by his clothes, during the winter 1947 PGA Tour.

The rainbow ducks behind a cloud and hides its face in shame.
The redbird, bluebird, and thrush look sordid, dull, and tame.
The pelican, with startled look, deserts the fish at sea,
When J. Demaret takes his stand upon the starting tee.

Green, blue, and crimson, pink and gold, with purple on the side,
He makes surrounding flower growth look drab, and even snide,
In one quick look at blazing flame, the rosebuds fade and fall,
But better still above the rest—the guy can hit that ball.

Rice then described Demaret preparing his wardrobe for the return to the PGA Tour. "Being a good-looking, colorful fellow, in order to offset the drabness of training and hard work, Jimmy laid in a supply of green, blue, purple, crimson, and orange golf caps that looked like young balloons. He also added a supply of yellow, green, and crimson coats and sweaters, plus multicolored trousers to keep the ensemble in proper order.

"He was the only fellow on the golf course you could recognize two miles away, a human rainbow in action," Rice wrote.

Rice quotes Demaret on how he had prepared for competition again. What he said contradicts the idea that Demaret never worked on his game. "After being away from golf for so long it took me some time to get my swing going. I found my timing way off. I also found it hard to keep concentrating. I might be all right for 18 holes and turn in a 67 or a 68, but I couldn't keep it up for 72 holes. This happened to most of the golfers who had been in the service. My judgment of distance was bad or spotty. But I had made up my mind to work and train and practice. As a result, I now am hitting the ball as well as I ever did, even during the year I won nine tournaments out of eleven starts. It has taken me more than a year to get my confidence back, but I feel much better about things now."

The Rice article on Demaret ends with more fanciful references to his attire, and an endorsement of his stature as a player. "It is reported that cardinals, bluebirds, and mockingbirds follow him around the course to get the latest in attire and voice. I would not know about that. For as gaudy as his raiment is, I'd rather watch his swing. There certainly isn't another fellow in golf who is better liked, both by players and galleries."

Demaret ended his best year on the PGA Tour in 1947 as both the leading money winner and winner of the Vardon Trophy, playing 88 rounds with an average of 69.75. Demaret's six wins that year were surpassed by Hogan who had seven. The two players partnered twice for victories in four-ball tournaments. Demaret finished fourth or better 18 times during the year, including being runner-up for the Richmond Open, San Antonio Open, Columbus Invitational, Albuquerque Open, Atlanta Open, and the Orlando Open. He also played on the Ryder Cup team.

The Houston Open in May of 1947 had amateur Whitey Sturman in the field. There were 42 pros and 33 amateurs in the field that year. Demaret was the godfather for Whitey's son, John Sturman, and whenever the pros came to San Antonio, where the Sturmans lived, they visited the Sturman home. The field for the event had a large number of people who in one way or another had a connection to Demaret. Amateur Jack Selman would become head professional after Milton Demaret in 1965 at Brae Burn Country Club. Amateur Tom Burke was Jack Burke Sr.'s nephew. Dick Forester had been hired by Demaret to work at River Oaks and he followed Demaret as head professional there. Milton Demaret was Jimmy's brother. George Fazio assisted with the design of the Jackrabbit Course at Champions. Tony Penna helped Demaret get an endorsement contract with MacGregor. Ben Hogan was Demaret's four-ball event partner.

When he won the Miami Open in December of 1947 Demaret shot a six-under-par 64 in the second round of the event, out in 33 and back in 31. He claimed to be nervous during the round. "I play best when I'm nervous and the tension is mounting," he said at the time. "I get a birdie, then hope for two, then three. As they pile up the tension rolls up and keeps rolling. If it breaks I'm a goner."

Even with this impressive links performance, Demaret's clothes still attracted primary attention. Lester Rice, a sportswriter of the time, described Demaret: "He's a sartorial sunset. His is the flamboyant love of the gypsy for flashing and crashing colors. Bright greens and reds or whatever howling hues happen to intrigue his regard he flaunts with the devil-may-care of a vagabond."

While the dollar amounts earned by PGA Tour professionals during the 1940s are minor in comparison with today's purses, even with inflation factored in, Demaret's standing in the money earnings during the 1940s illustrates how well he was doing each year. In 1941 he finished the year seventh on the money list. He wasn't in the top 10 in money winning in 1942, the PGA Tour was dormant during 1943, and it would not be until 1946 that Demaret again entered the top 10 list among money winners, when he placed fourth. He won the money title in 1947, placed third on the list in 1948, fifth in 1949, seventh in 1950. He didn't place among the top 10 again in his career, but he did finish 20th on the list in 1956 and 13th in 1957, a year he won three PGA Tour events.

Burkes and Demarets played in events other than the times Jack and Jimmy played in the same competition. In 1948 the Houston Golf Association Festival featured five different championships for the city. The amateur champion was Tommy Burke Jr., nephew of Jack

Burke Sr. and son of club professional Tommy Burke. Milton Demaret, Jimmy's brother, in the professional division took the eventual winner Butch Krueger to 37 holes before losing. The August 4, 1948 issue of *Golf World* magazine featured a photo of Milton playing with members at Brae Burn Country Club, where Milton was head professional. In the next week's issue the magazine ran an ad announcing that LPGA founding member Louise Suggs was joining the advisory and technical staff of *Golf World,* joining a group that included Jimmy Demaret.

Early in the 1948 golf season Demaret eliminated himself from any chance of repeating as winner of the Vardon Trophy, which he had won in 1947. In February at the New Orleans Open after he played the eighth hole he picked up his ball and withdrew from the tournament. The tournament committee chairperson for The PGA, George Schneiter, released a statement on the matter. "The PGA rules say every round started must be completed for a player to get the Vardon Trophy," Schneiter said. "I've been charged with enforcing the rules, and I have to declare Jimmy ineligible."

Demaret was one of several pros entered in the New Orleans event who had been upset that Fred Haas Jr. apparently was playing with clubs whose grooves were improperly scored. At the time, Schneiter said that he had inspected the clubs and approved them. How Demaret's protest of picking up his ball and withdrawing from the tournament at all punished Haas, Schneiter, or anyone but himself is not known.

Lew Worsham partnered with Demaret for the 1949 Miami Four-Ball event. The team made it to the semifinals of the match play tournament, winning $400 for their efforts.

Demaret finished second to Sam Snead in the Texas Open in February of 1950 by one stroke. Snead had to shoot final rounds of successive 63s in order to beat Demaret. The beginning of the golf season in 1950 was notable for three golfers each winning three tour events 16 weeks into the year. The three were Demaret, Sam Snead, and Jack Burke Jr. The next time that happened was not until 2003 when

Davis Love III, Mike Weir, and Tiger Woods each won three times early in the season.

The Associated Press reported on April 1, 1950 that 11 pros, including Demaret, Hogan, Middlecoff, and Snead were organizing as the Professional Golf Players Division of The PGA to operate the PGA Tour. One week later the situation was resolved by the players accepting four seats on The PGA's tournament committee, providing them some representation in the operations of the tour. However distracting the dispute might have been, Demaret finished that week by winning his third Masters on April 9, becoming the first player to earn three of the titles.

The *Saturday Evening Post,* then one of the most popular magazines in America, in its issue of June 10, 1950 ran an article by Charley Price called "Golf's Gorgeous Jester." Price described Demaret: "Nice-looking, although too blue-eyed and apple-cheeked to be labeled handsome, Demaret is the warmest, most human contact between the high-powered pros and the one-cylinder amateurs who pay to see them play. He is endlessly engaged in shaking hands, slapping backs, and stroking children's heads. Almost singlehanded he puts over the idea that big-shot pros are human, when most of the others are doing their best to spoil the illusion.

"Demaret's build gives him a low center of gravity, making it very easy for him to keep his balance even in the highest of winds. Many experts say he is the greatest foul-weather player on record—a vital attribute, since tournament scheduling is so tight that it is seldom possible to call off a round no matter how bad the playing conditions.

"Because of his odd physique, Jimmy addresses the ball with his feet very close together and a pronounced sitting-down effect, and hits full drives with a stance that most golfers employ on niblick pitches. He can drive almost as well on one foot as on two. He delivers his power through a pair of tremendously strong hands attached to wrists that look like the driveshaft of a limousine. His swing looks simple—a whiplash action with the arms and an almost imperceptible weight shift."

Demaret with Bob Hope, on the right, and Milton Demaret, 3rd from right, and members at Brae Burn Country Club at a function in the 1950s. (courtesy of Brae Burn Country Club)

Price went on to offer an insight into why Demaret did so well in tournament golf: "He does well at almost any kind of athletic activity, and at nonathletic games, too. He plays gin rummy, chess, checkers, dominoes, table tennis, and even bocce ball with great skill. It is a natural gamesmanship that he takes onto the golf course, and he capitalizes more on tactical soundness and accuracy than on sheer power."

By 1950, at age 40, Demaret had enjoyed considerable success as a professional golfer for more than 12 years. He explained to Price what the game of golf had done for him: "Golf took young kids like Byron Nelson and Ben Hogan and myself out of the caddie ranks and gave us money and a little bit of fame and let us live in the tall cotton. I carried so many bags back in the old days my right shoulder was lower than my left, and all I ever got in return was a few laughs. It was fighting, cheating, gambling, and a couple of times I saw a knifing. That's fine scenery for a 13-year-old mind, but it all paid off. Believe me, it's sweeter now, and there's lots more laughs."

CHAPTER 3

CHANGING GEARS

"Smoothie Man"

◆ ◆ ◆

After the success of the five years between 1946 and 1950, Demaret began to cut back on his tour schedule. He had a remarkable 12 victories in professional tournaments after age 40, but he entered fewer events and his interests included many activities beyond golf. By 1954 he described himself as a "semi-tour" player, participating in some of the tour events but not all of them. He still managed 15 top 25 finishes in tournaments during 1951, showing that the ability was still there, but he limited his play compared to the previous five years.

There were several reasons for this. With his third Masters victory in 1950, he had clearly established himself as one of the best golfers of his era. He had won 16 events over the past five years, the Vardon Trophy, and the money earnings title for 1947. At the age of 40, he had accomplished what he wanted to do in golf, and if he did not have U.S. Open or PGA Championship titles, he had competed sufficiently well in those events enough times to confirm his playing ability.

He was also involved in a variety of ventures beyond tournament golf. He was an advisor and endorser of golf clubs for MacGregor Sporting Goods Company, a role he had maintained for 13 years. In the early 1950s he invested in First Flight, a golf equipment manufacturing company in Chattanooga, Tennessee. He was a partner in the Burke-Harris Uniform Company in Houston. He also developed a relationship with the Palm Beach Company, to promote their clothes. He had many friends in the business community in Houston and elsewhere who constantly offered him new opportunities. After several years of being associated with the Ojai Valley Inn, he began a club affiliation with the Concord Hotel at Kiamesha Lake, New York where he was touring professional, and he spent part of the year playing golf with his celebrity friends, fellow tour professionals, and hotel guests.

He had also witnessed the consequences of the unfortunate and nearly fatal car accident of his friend Ben Hogan. Demaret may have felt that he was fortunate not to have met the same fate himself. Traveling conditions were still difficult for golf professionals driving from event to event on two lane roads, and the travel was tiring at best, dangerous at worst. Demaret was already interested in becoming a better pilot to make travel more convenient, something he would accomplish in a few years.

Life magazine, whose circulation at the time was over 5 million, had a feature story in its May 14, 1951 issue on Jimmy Demaret, but it wasn't a sports story. Under a heading of "Fashion" in the magazine's table of contents was a story titled "Best-Dressed Golfer." On the jacket of this book is the full-page color photo of Demaret with some of his wardrobe on display that ran with the article.

The story describes the scope of Demaret's collection of clothes: "Not only does he design and promote colorful golf clothes himself, but he has set a brilliant example in his own wardrobe, almost all of which he gets free....Altogether it consists of some 75 pairs of Technicolored slacks, 60 custom-made sports jackets, 150 shirts, 40 pairs of Demaret-styled shoes, and a current collection of 35 caps. He likes hats but finds it hard to hang onto them since souvenir hunters have made off with more than 1,000, including one that was a present from ex-King Carol of Romania." The article shows five photos of Jimmy modeling some of his hat collection, two of which had been crocheted by his mother-in-law. She also made him matching head covers for his woods.

Concord Hotel in the 1950s. (courtesy of John Parker)

One of the stores where Demaret bought his clothes in Houston was Harold's in the Heights, which was started by Harold Wiesenthal and his brother Milton. Harold became a member at Champions Golf Club, and, in 1969, he served on the attire committee for the U.S. Open held at Champions. He recalled being with Demaret one day at Memorial Golf Club when he was leaving the clubhouse. Demaret paused to shake the hands of a group of caddies gathered nearby and then he shook hands with some of the golfers. "He treated everybody the same way," said Harold. "He was good to people wherever he went."

Demaret's affiliation with the Concord Hotel at Kiamesha Lake, New York began in 1951. He spoke about his relationship with the Concord for an article done by Bob Rule in the *Houston Chronicle* in 1964. "I've been with Concord for 14 years and have never had a contract," Demaret said. "It has been a very fine association for me. I

L-R: Buddy Hackett, Demaret, Jack Burke Jr., Sam Snead, Ben Hogan, and Billy Eckstine at the Concord. (courtesy of John Parker)

usually spend about four to five months a year there, but recently I've just been in and out. I'm spending more time here at Champions."

Demaret was the touring pro representing the Concord, which was located about 100 miles northwest of New York City. John Parker, great-grandson of the founder of the hotel, Arthur Winarick, recalls that from end to end, you could walk inside the complex for one-half mile. The dining room seated 5,000. Surrounded by 3,000 chaise lounge chairs, the swimming pool covered an acre. A 200-foot-long bar stretched along a wall of the Night Owl Lounge. For his frequent visits to the hotel Demaret maintained an apartment above the golf pro shop.

The Concord had opened in 1939, but it began its era of national fame after World War II, attracting the best entertainers and expanding the hotel's facilities into one of the largest resort complexes on

Joe Finger, Tommy Bolt, and Demaret at the Concord Hotel. (courtesy of Joe Finger)

the East Coast. The property became so popular that it needed a second golf course. Demaret brought in his friend Joe Finger to do the design work with input from him and Jack Burke. Finger had attended Rice University in the 1930s and played on the golf team, which practiced at Brae Burn Country Club, and had Demaret as a coach.

Finger remembered Demaret saying to him in regard to golf course design that "no one ever brags about how easy his golf course is." The initial discussions about the golf course at the Concord that would be called the Monster were in 1959, but it was 1961 when the construction began, with the official opening in 1963. Tommy Bolt, Bob Rosburg, Miller Barber, Demaret and Burke were among the pros on hand for the grand opening. The course gained immediate recognition as being among the most difficult in the U.S. and soon was ranked by *Golf Digest* among the top 100 courses.

One episode in his tour activity during 1951 illustrates how disengaged Demaret had become with the life of a traveling professional, while at the same time showing how popular he was. An incident which started with Demaret being fined by The PGA of America ended with Demaret being celebrated with testimonial dinners and the United States State Department praising his efforts in support of America's Good Neighbor Policy.

On Tuesday morning, February 20, 1951 the *Los Angeles Times* ran a large headline on the front page of its sports section:

Demaret Blasts Horton Smith in
PGA Squabble; Threatens to Sue

The accompanying story explained that Demaret had been fined $500 by The PGA of America as a result of playing in an event in Mexico "while the Rio Grande Valley Open was in progress at Harlingen, Tex." Fined along with Demaret were his fellow pros Vic Ghezzi, who was assessed a $350 penalty, and Al Besselink, fined $200, as were Morris Williams, Stan Dundas, George Kinsman Jr., Willie Polumbo, Nick Lazori, and Ansel Snow.

In defending himself Demaret said: "The tournament committee knew that we were going to play in Mexico as early as the Los Angeles Open, had a meeting with us and representatives from Mexico at Phoenix and again at San Antonio.

"Not one of us was committed to play in Harlingen. I never broke a commitment in my life."

Before leaving for the Mexican National Open Demaret was informed that he was at risk of being fined, because the event in Mexico was not a "major championship" and that the tournament was not cosponsored by The PGA. He was defiant in his response: "The PGA is out of line to say the Mexico Open is not a championship tournament. Might as well tell the British they don't have a national championship. The Mexico tournament has drawn Roberto de Vicenzo from Argentina. Would he be going there to play if it was not a championship tournament? Where is our Good Neighbor Policy?"

Demaret, in the tam hat, on the front of a postcard for the Concord Hotel.

Demaret hits a shot during the construction of "The Monster" course at the Concord Hotel, while Ray Parker, the hotel manager, and Joe Finger, the course designer, watch. (courtesy of Joe Finger)

A decade later the same rule affected Arnold Palmer and even several international players when the Canada Cup matches conflicted with a PGA Tour event in Memphis, Tennessee. Arnold Palmer, selected to play on the American team, was prohibited from participating in the Canada Cup in 1961, and Demaret substituted for him in the matches.

The response in the golf community to the 1951 incident was in favor of Demaret and the other pros that had been fined. The issue of controlling where the professionals could play had long been a divisive one between the tour players and The PGA of America, and it was among the issues that led to the separation of the PGA Tour from The PGA of America in the late 1960s.

Wealthy Houston oilman and owner of the Shamrock Hotel Glenn McCarthy paid the $1,100 in fines levied against the golfers who were going to play in the Houston Open the week the fines were announced. The PGA had said that the players would be suspended from PGA events until the fines were paid. When the defiant Demaret was presented a check at Memorial Park Golf Course prior to the start of the Houston Open PGA event on February 23, he was wearing a sombrero and serape and carrying American and Mexican flags.

The saga continued. In March, *Golfista Mexicano,* the official paper of De La Asociacion Mexicana De Professional De Golf, issued a statement in regard to the incident: "The PGA has no right to classify our National Open tournament. We, therefore, discard as null and void its preposterous decision to the effect that our tournament is not a major tournament. We have never tried to place ourselves above others, but we do not tolerate that anyone places himself or tries to place himself above the highest golfing Mexican authority which represents organized golf in Mexico."

Vic Ghezzi was scratched from the Miami Beach Open field in early march because he had not paid the fine for going to Mexico levied by The PGA. In protest, Demaret withdrew from the event.

The issue subsequently escalated into an international matter. The Mexican government perceived The PGA's reaction to the golfers' trip to their country as an insult. When the tournament had been held in February, Mexican President Miguel Aleman had his picture taken standing between Demaret and Roberto de Vicenzo. The United States government was then compelled to respond to the complaint from Mexico. By May it was announced that Demaret on June 2 would receive a citation from the State Department of the United States for making an outstanding contribution to the Good Neighbor Policy of the United States. In New York on June 5, Demaret was the guest of honor for a testimonial dinner sponsored by sports writers Grantland Rice and Red Smith, the president of the New York Yankees Dan Topping, former U.S. Open champion Craig Wood, and former PGA tournament director Fred Corcoran. For the dinner in New York President Truman and United States Attorney General McGrath sent Demaret an "Award of Merit" for helping international relations. As if Demaret needed further confirmation of how much people liked him, in August of 1951 Demaret was given another testimonial dinner, this time in Houston at Sorrento's restaurant.

Another international complication developed in July of 1951 regarding the British Open. Somehow the Royal & Ancient Golf Club understood that several American players were going to participate that year, but the club was never officially notified that the players would not compete. The *London Daily Mail* reported what happened when the players did not appear for their assigned tee times: "Failure of the Americans—Bulla, Demaret, McHale, Coe, and Riegel (to appear) led to a rather farcical rite being enacted on the first tee. Each time they were due to start their names were called out and formal scratching took place only when they failed to respond. It was quite humorous to all concerned except their partners, who, in each instance, had to attend on the first tee and then walk back to the clubhouse to wait, before they could be set into the draw with other partners." No explanation was given as to the origin of the confusion about whether the players were scheduled to play.

One of Demaret's most remarkable shots happened in the 1951 World Championship of Golf, played at Chicago's Tam O'Shanter in August that year. Demaret led the event by five strokes after the third round, after shooting 67-69-66. The 66 was achieved with the help of one of his most memorable shots. On the 445-yard, fourth hole in the third round, his drive settled in the rough and under a tree. He was able to take a full swing at the ball, watched it approach the green 200 yards away, and then heard the wild cheers when the ball went in the hole for an eagle two. After playing so well the first three days he shot a 74 on Sunday to lose to Ben Hogan by three shots.

Topping off his year of international controversy, Demaret once again showed how well he could take his game on the road by winning the fourth annual Havana Open in December of 1951. He shot 67, 72, 67, 69 to win the event by one stroke over runner-up Bob Toski. Also participating from the PGA Tour were Claude Harmon, Toney Penna, Doug Ford, Lew Worsham, and Julius Boros.

The Bing Crosby Pro-Am was one of Jimmy Demaret's favorite events on the pro tour. Though famous for its current setting at Pebble Beach where the event was moved for the January 1947 tournament, it began in 1937 at Rancho Santa Fe in San Diego County, near where Bing Crosby had a ranch as well as involvement in the Del Mar horse racetrack. Demaret had become friends with Crosby and Bob Hope from his participation in the Los Angeles Open.

The format of the event was initially only two rounds of play. When it resumed play in 1947 after the hiatus for the war and the move to the Monterey Peninsula, the format was extended to three rounds, and finally to four rounds in 1958, the first year the event was televised.

Demaret had a third-place finish in 1938, and tied for fourth in 1941, when 319 players participated, requiring two days to finish the first round. In 1947 he tied for fifth. The tournament had no provision for a play-off in case of a tie for first, and George Fazio and Ed Furgol were named cochampions that year. In 1948 Demaret tied for sixth, and he placed third in 1949. In the 1951 event, Phil Harris, who became good friends with Demaret in later years and would call him nearly every day at Champions, on the 17th hole of the final round sank a 90-foot putt. The putt contributed to the win by Harris and his pro partner Dutch Harrison in the pro-am division of the tournament.

Bing Crosby and Demaret. (courtesy of Jack Treece)

Crosby and Demaret. (courtesy of The PGA of America)

Bad weather afflicted the 1952 event, but Demaret prevailed in the rain-shortened tournament. "The weather was more fit for Johnny Weissmuller's swimming than my 5-iron," Demaret said. "But for $2,500 I can stand a little moisture." His payment was $2,000 for winning the professional division and $500 for a third-place finish in the pro-am with partner Bob Hope. Later that evening at the awards ceremony, Demaret went to the stage to sing a duet with Monica Lewis and trade jokes with comedian Buddy Hackett.

That year Crosby presented Demaret with head covers for his woods made of mink with ermine tassels. To complement these Demaret added mink-lined playing gloves to his outfit.

One of the courses used at that time for playing the Crosby was Cypress Point. Demaret said of the 16th hole on the course, "The nearest point of relief is Honolulu."

Whatever problems Demaret had with The PGA of America in 1951 must have been resolved by 1952. Demaret traveled to Australia in 1952 for the Lakes Cup Matches between teams representing The PGA of America and Australia. Participating in the trip with Demaret were fellow professionals Lloyd Mangrum, Ed "Porky" Oliver, and Jim Turnesa. The matches had first been held in Australia in 1934, then repeated in Long Beach, California in 1935, but were then suspended. The format was one day of foursome matches, with another day of singles, both at 36 holes. The American team won in 1952 by a score of 7-5, with the full program of matches repeated both in Sydney and Melbourne. The four Americans stayed in Australia for a month and participated in other tournaments and exhibitions.

The sponsor for the Lakes Cup was Australian Bill Walkley, chairman of the board of an oil firm. When the Lakes Cup was over, Demaret requested that his prize money be awarded to him as oil stock. The first time they drilled they struck oil.

Demaret added two more PGA Tour wins to his resume during 1952, at the Crosby and then the National Celebrities Tournament in August. He managed eight top 10 finishes for the year. The next year he won two more events, this time at the Thunderbird Pro-Am and the La Gorce Pro-Am, but neither was an official PGA Tour event at

Demaret on the left with Crosby. (courtesy of The PGA of America)

Demaret, on the right, with Perry Como and models at the 1952 National Celebrities Tournament. (courtesy of The PGA of America)

the time. When Demaret won the Thunderbird in 1957 it had become an official PGA Tour event.

On tour in 1954, Demaret placed in the top 10 only three times, his lowest number since 1945 when he only had the opportunity to play in six events. His performance in 1955 was not much better. Entering 11 events, he placed in the top 10 three times.

Jack Burke had the best year of his career in 1956, winning two majors and 10 times finishing in the top 10 on the PGA Tour. The highlights of the year were his victories at the Masters and The PGA Championship, then still played as a match play event. His accomplishments even got him into the syndicated newspaper feature "Ripley's Believe It or Not." "A chip off the old block," read the feature. "Jack Burke Jr., son of the famous professional, Jack Burke, won both the Masters and PGA Tournaments in 1956, the second player in history to perform this feat." The article also noted that "Burke shot a 69 at the age of 12 and qualified for the U.S. Open at the age of 16."

After the unproductive years of 1954 and 1955, Demaret reapplied himself to his golf game and at age 45 began playing well again on the PGA Tour. The June 1956 issue of *Golf Digest* featured Demaret on the cover with the tag line "Jimmy Demaret's Fabulous Career." The article describes Demaret as regaining his playing form of earlier years, claiming that he was "playing golf good enough to win any tournament in the world. Demaret, 46 on May 10, is actually making a comeback for he hasn't done too much since 1950, when he won his third Masters championship and $16,268 to rank seventh among the pros. Last year, for instance, he played in only a few events and cashed just $4,684 worth of prize money checks.

"Golf's goodwill ambassador hadn't won a tournament since the 1953 National Celebrities until he walked off with all the marbles at Palm Springs this year. Although he beat out Cary Middlecoff by only one stroke with his superb 269, Demaret was eight swings ahead of the next competitor, young Gene Littler.

"Ole' Jim credits his new lease on life to two things—a slower swing and a tighter putting grip."

Demaret had apparently identified exactly what was wrong with his golf swing and corrected the problem. "I've tried to slow down my swing and it has helped me a lot," he told Dick Peebles, sports editor of the *San Antonio Express.* "I discovered I was hurrying it. I believe when a fellow gets older he loses his nerve control. You have to compensate for that. What I try to do is see the club head hit the ball. When I do that, I know I've hit a good shot."

Even his putting had undergone a transformation. "I used to putt with a relaxed, loose grip. But I discovered that I was tightening my hold on the putter just before I stroked the ball. That's nerve control again. It didn't matter too much on long putts, but I was missing the four and five footers that you have to make to win tournaments."

In the same issue the magazine had an article previewing the U.S. Open, to be held at Oak Hill in Rochester, NY that year. A handicap chart predicts the players' prospects of winning and Demaret is

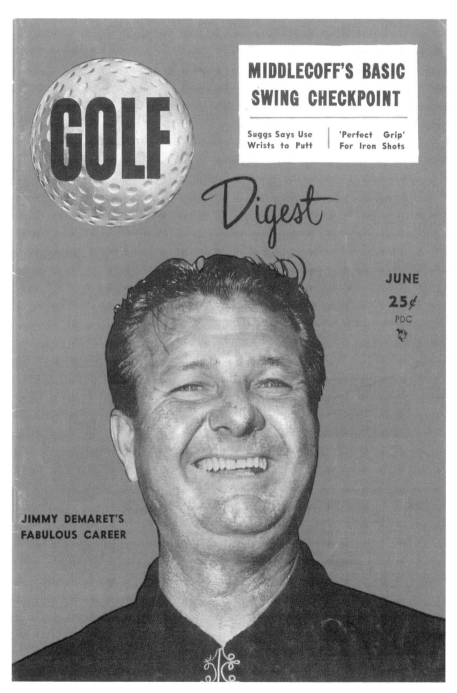

Golf Digest, *June of 1956.*

shown at number 10 on the list with 17:1 odds, with the comment that he was "gaining second breath." The magazine had Jack Burke as the second best prospect at 4:1 odds. Burke went on to win The PGA Championship a month later, held July 20–24 that year.

In a year when Demaret captured three victories on tour, 1957, he also played well enough to finish in third place in both the Masters and the U.S. Open. His performance in the Open that year was his best other than his runner-up finish to Hogan in 1948. He started the year by winning the Thunderbird Invitational. Then in a stretch of 13 straight events he placed no lower than tied for eighth, including winning the Baton Rouge Open and the Arlington Open. He added another four top 10 finishes the rest of the year.

He had reached age 47 in May of 1957, but he had a renewed sense of commitment to his golf. During 1955 he had endured an illness that was first thought to be cancer, but fortunately was not. As a result he rededicated himself to playing well, and his play in 1956 and 1957 further confirmed his ability. Speaking in June of 1957 at the U.S. Open about his regained interest in the game he said: "My attitude is the difference. I'm more serious. I decided I wanted to prove a few things to myself a few years ago. I realized I didn't have too much time left."

Demaret and Snead traveled to Japan in October 1957 to represent America in the Canada Cup matches. The Japanese were very impressed with Snead's long drives. "Mr. Sam Snead is big hitter," said one fan. "Ball go very far." Demaret made a different impression on the fans. "He is really smoothie man," said a Japanese fan about Demaret. "Easy swing, ball go very straight and very close to hole."

The Houston Open provides a good case for the durability of Jimmy Demaret's golf skills and competitive spirit. In 1957 the event was played February 21–25, a year when the 26-year-old Arnold Palmer shot 67-72-71-69 in winning the event. Demaret shot 68-73-68-73 to finish in fourth place. His 68 in the third round gave him a total one stroke ahead of Palmer, who was 20 years his junior. The Memorial Park Golf Course hosting the event that year played to 7,212 yards, a fair test of golf even by post-titanium and enhanced golf ball standards.

The next year Demaret finished tied for fourth. From 1959 through 1964 Demaret made the cut in the event and finished T-45, T-18, T-38, T-68, T-19, and 13th. His 13th place finish in 1964 was accomplished by scores of 70-72-70-72 on the Sharpstown Country Club course measuring 7,201 yards. The April event that year was one month prior to his 54th birthday. The event became the Houston Champions International in 1966, hosted by Champions Golf Club, which had the event through 1968, then the club hosted the U.S. Open in 1969, and the PGA Tour event stopped there again for 1970 and 1971. The 1970 Houston Champions International is notable for the 59-year-old Ben Hogan shooting 71-75-71-70 to finish tied for ninth.

After his stellar year of 1957, in 1958 Demaret reduced his tournament participation to 10 events. Champions Golf Club was in development and required most of his time. He still managed to place in the top 25 nine times, including a second and a third, and in 1959 he had two second-place finishes. He continued to have top 25 finishes ever year on tour through 1964.

Demaret was asked in 1961 to fill in for Arnold Palmer in the Canada Cup matches. Palmer and Sam Snead had been selected to represent the United States in the matches to be held in Puerto Rico, which would feature two-man teams from several nations, an event that had first been held in 1953, and then in 1966 was renamed the World Cup. Demaret played on the United States team with Sam Snead in 1954. The Canada Cup eventually became part of the series of four events held each year that are part of the world championship series, including the Andersen Consulting Match Play Championship, the NEC Invitational, and the American Express Championship.

Two weeks prior to the event, in 1961, Palmer was informed that due to a PGA rule that required him to participate in the PGA Tournament in Memphis, he could not participate in the Canada Cup. The rules further prevented foreign players on the United States PGA Tour from competing in the event, which meant that Gary Player could not represent South Africa and Stan Leonard could not represent Canada. They were replaced by Harold Henning and Al Johnston.

Snead, at 16-under-par for four rounds, and Demaret, at even par, made a good team, winning the event.

Demaret's last real shot at winning a PGA Tour event, at age 53, came about unexpectedly in February of 1964 at the Palm Springs Classic in California. The event included Jack Nicklaus, Billy Casper, Don January, Julius Boros, and other tour stars of the time. Though he started with a 75, Demaret, playing as a favor to Bob Hope who was the tournament's host, put together a 68 and a 67 in the next two rounds to get into contention, then added a 72 in the five-round event, but Casper and Chuck Courney were in the lead going into the final round. On a day when the entire field battled a sandstorm, Demaret managed a 71 and Tommy Jacobs shot a 70 to tie, while Casper and Courney soared to a 77 and a 76, respectively. Demaret missed a 30-inch putt on the final hole of regulation play that would have won him the tournament. A play-off began with the crowd cheering Demaret with "Come on, Grandpa." After both players bogeyed the first play-off hole, Jacobs won the event with a par 3 on the next hole to Demaret's bogey. Eleven years before, Demaret had won at Palm Springs when he shot 69, 65, and 67 in the final three rounds to beat Jim Turnesa by two strokes.

In April of 1964, Demaret played an exhibition match at Merion Golf Club outside Philadelphia with Ray Bolger, famous for his portrayal of the scarecrow seeking a heart in the movie *The Wizard of Oz,* Arnold Palmer, fresh from his fourth Masters victory, and Dwight Eisenhower, three years out of office as president. The exhibition was to benefit the Heart Association of Southeastern Pennsylvania, and was Eisenhower's only public golf performance.

Eisenhower was up to the occasion, and Palmer later claimed that "the General carried me," which was not an exaggeration. The match was an alternate shot format and on the first green Ike rolled in a seven-footer for a birdie for the Palmer-Eisenhower team. Ike chipped to two feet from the cup on the eighth hole to assist on the birdie they made there. Even though the match was officially over by the 16th hole, when they were three and two over the Demaret-

Bolger team, they played out the final two holes. As if to show that he always took his golf seriously, at 17 Ike rolled in a 45-foot putt, eliciting an enormous roar from the gallery.

Shell's Wonderful World of Golf television show aired a match in February of 1966 between Demaret and Sam Snead that had been filmed at Eisenhower Golf Course at the U.S. Air Force Academy outside Colorado Springs, Colorado. Demaret's first victory on the PGA Tour had been in the San Francisco match play event in 1938 when he defeated Snead in the finals. In the previous 10 years they had teamed together in the Canada Cup matches. By late 1965, when the Shell match with Snead was filmed, Demaret was six years into retirement from being active on the PGA Tour, although he had nearly won at Palm Springs less than two years before. Snead won his last regular PGA Tour victory in 1965 at the Greater Greensboro Open, just before his 53rd birthday.

The day of the Shell match was sunny, but as the program host George Rogers pointed out, there had been rain two days previously and a light snow the day before, leaving the Robert Trent Jones Sr. layout wet and playing long. The weather turned colder as the day progressed, with even the announcer wearing a topcoat. The winner of the match was to receive $7,000 and the loser $3,000, and the two golfers always took playing for money seriously. Dow Finsterwald, who lived in the area, came out to follow the match.

Demaret's first putt of the round from 40 feet hit the hole and spun out. On the third hole, Demaret put his approach shot in a greenside bunker, leaving himself 50 feet to the hole. He put his bunker shot a foot from the hole. By the turn, Demaret was two over par and Snead was even. On the back nine the temperature began to drop and both the golfers and the gallery looked uncomfortable. By 18, Demaret could be seen blowing on his hands to warm them prior to his tee shot. He finished at four over par to Snead's two over par. Both players had made several putts from more than eight feet, and despite the weather conditions both managed to display the level of play that had won them over 100 PGA Tour victories combined. Six years earlier Demaret had prevailed against Snead in May 1960 in a round-robin all-star golf tournament at the Yorba Linda Country Club in California, not an official PGA Tour event.

Demaret's love for competitive golf never left him. He did have a lot of pride about his play and the idea of playing at a level less than he felt was his standard wasn't acceptable to him. For someone of his age in the 1960s there was no PGA Senior Tour, now known as the Champions Tour. In fact, Demaret was one of the people who helped make that happen by starting the Legends of Golf event in 1978.

He had spoken to reporter Emmet Collins in 1957 about how he felt about golf: "Sure I smile, and sure, I talk to the gallery. But when I make a bad shot, don't think that it doesn't hurt me inside. You bet it kills me inside. I'm a competitor and I like to win. I've always been that way. I have to admit, I never think of the money. Even when I was younger and had nothing and needed money, I didn't think about it.

"But you begin to smell that title and you want to win. Nobody in this game wants to win like I do. There's no sense in playing golf unless you feel that way."

CHAPTER 4

THE MAJORS AND THE RYDER CUP

"All That Is Great in Golf"

◆ ◆ ◆

THE MASTERS

His victory in the San Francisco Match Play event in 1938 and then the 1939 Los Angeles Open earned Demaret an invitation to the 1939 Masters. Since 1935 he had been a participant in The PGA Championship, and since 1936 in the U.S. Open, with his T-16 finish that year being his best performance in these events.

In the second round of the 1939 Masters, Demaret shot an 81, eventually finishing tied for 33rd place with the tournament's founder and host, Bobby Jones. They were joined by Walter Hagen, then way past his prime but still an important figure in the world of golf. Demaret would be compared to Hagen throughout his career. When Demaret finished tied for 33rd that year he was way out of the money, which was paid to only the top 12 contestants and ties.

When he arrived for the 1940 Masters he was one of the favorites to win, having won five events on the tour from January through March. He had also won two pro-am events in Florida that were not on the official PGA schedule, but that earned him $5,000. First place in the Masters offered $1,500 at the time. Before the tournament began, the betting oddsmakers put Ralph Guldahl, the previous year's champion, at 6 to 1. Ben Hogan shared the same odds for victory. Demaret was set at 8 to 1 and Byron Nelson at 9 to 1. Bobby Jones, 10 years into his retirement from competitive golf in 1930, had a practice round of 66 that was the biggest news prior to Thursday.

Jack Burke Jr. later described why Demaret had a golf game that fit well with Augusta National: "He was a phenomenal driver of the ball, never far off-line. He teed it real low, and hit the ball close to the ground the way most players of his time did. Also, the greens at Augusta were fast and Jimmy was a phenomenal putter on fast greens because he used a short stroke. Just right for Augusta."

Byron Nelson said about Demaret at Augusta: "In those years, the greens at Augusta were not only fast, they also were very hard. Jimmy played a left-to-right iron shot that landed softly, so he could hold those greens."

Lloyd Mangrum's record-breaking 64 on Thursday in 1940 overshadowed Demaret's fine round of 67, which included a 30 on the back nine after an unpromising front nine of 37. The *New York Times* reported on Demaret's back nine score: "That 30 alone is worthy of more than mere mention, for it eclipsed by one shot the previous nine-hole mark of Willie MacFarlane in the United States Open at Worcester in 1925 and equaled the record made by Francis Ouimet when he played George Voight in the United States Amateur at Baltimore."

Three putts on the second and eighth holes contributed to Demaret's problems on the front nine. The *New York Times* described the rest of the round: "But once he got started on the second nine there was no stopping him. The fireworks started when he fired a No. 1 iron up to within a yard of the flag on the 10th hole and rolled in the putt for his first birdie of the round. On the 11th he rammed a 30-footer in for another birdie and then, after going over the green on his tee shot to the short 12th and saving himself by getting down in two for a par, he rolled off four more birdies in the next six holes.

"He produced a birdie 4 on the 13th with a 25 footer after being short on his second shot, had a regulation 4 on the 14th, exploded a buried ball out of the mud on the 15th and bowled in a 50-foot putt, and another good-sized one for a deuce on the short 16th, [145 yards

Demaret shows off his hat after the 1940 Masters to Grantland Rice on the left and Charles Bartlett on the right. (Ed Bernd Sr., courtesy of Rob Sommers)

at the time], and pitched up to within five feet and holed out for a birdie 3 on the 17th.

"And he almost got a 3 on the 18th from a distance of 25 feet that would have brought him home in 29."

Demaret later described what he had to do to make the shot on 15 from the buried lie: "Showing complete fearlessness, I removed my red-and-blue suede shoes, rolled my chartreuse slacks up to my knees, and stepped into two feet of water to make the shot. I used a wedge and hit well. The ball sailed out and came down on the green." Seven years later, on the same hole, he would accomplish a similar shot in winning his second Masters.

On Friday, only amateur Marvin "Bud" Ward could manage to break 70, shooting a 68. Demaret shot 72 and Mangrum shot 75 to put them in a tie for the lead, with Nelson two shots back. Then

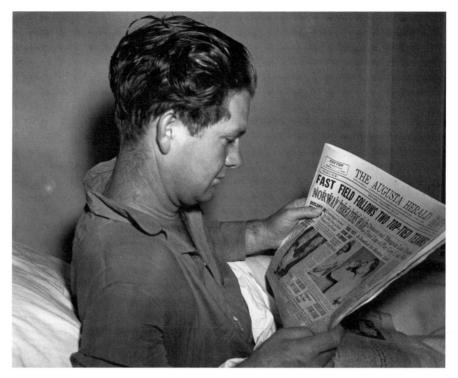

Demaret reads about himself in the 1940 Masters while recuperating in an Augusta hospital from a stomach ailment. (courtesy of Historic Golf Photos)

Demaret had to contend with a stomach ailment that put him in the hospital, where he was photographed reading a headline describing his tie for lead in the event. Despite being weak from the illness, Demaret edged into the lead after Saturday's round with his 70, while Mangrum came in at 71. Three players worthy of Demaret's attention made a move on Saturday, with Snead posting a 69, Craig Wood a 67, and Ben Hogan a 69.

Henry Picard, the 1938 Masters champion, four shots out of first after Saturday's round, was paired with Demaret on Sunday. Pairings were at the discretion of the tournament at that time, rather than the format of pairings based on the standings after each round. Picard faltered early in his round, bogeying the third through the fifth holes and finishing with a 75 after three straight rounds of 71.

Demaret played steady, but not spectacular, golf through his final round. He did not make a birdie until the 15th hole, when his third shot stopped inches from the hole, barely missing an eagle. He needed to get up and down from behind the green on 10, sank a five-footer for par on 11, and he parred in after the birdie on 15. But his 71 for the day was good enough for a commanding four shot win, with Mangrum holding on to finish second.

After the event, William Richardson in the *New York Times* described the Masters that year "a somewhat drab one because of the ease with which Demaret won it." However, Richardson may have spoken too soon about what Demaret accomplished. Demaret's bogey-free final round for the champion in the Masters has been equaled only three times from then through 2003. Hogan accomplished it in 1951, Doug Ford in 1957, and Mike Weir in 2003.

The win in the 1940 Masters and his five victories early in the golf year brought recognition from *Time* magazine. The article quoted him about his attitude of not taking the game too seriously: "When I start worrying over my shots and getting mad at myself, I'm going to give up tournament golf and go back to work."

In his next two Masters appearances Demaret was not a strong contender. In 1941 an opening round 77 was too much of a deficit to overcome, but he managed to finish tied for twelfth. In 1942 he started well with back-to-back 70s, only to finish with back-to-back 75s and end the event in sixth place. Then the war intervened for three years, stopping the tournament. The event restarted in 1946, with a field of only 51 amateurs and professionals. Another poor start for Demaret with a 75 put him too far behind to catch up, but he finished tied for fourth, which is exactly where, prior to the tournament, golf writer O.B. Keeler had placed him among those with a chance to win. Hogan, Nelson, and Snead were named by Keeler as the favorites.

On his way to winning the Masters in 1947 Demaret accomplished a shot that was considered so remarkable that Robert Sommers and Cal Brown featured it in their book *Great Shots* over four decades

Charlie Yates, a Georgia native who won the 1938 British Amateur Championship, congratulates Demaret on winning the 1940 Masters. Yates was low amateur in the event that year. (courtesy of Historic Golf Photos)

later. At that time the 15th hole at Augusta National played to 520 yards. It had been the site of Gene Sarazen's double-eagle in 1935, and nearly every year someone produced a sufficiently dramatic shot there to create a reputation for the hole as one of the best risk-and-reward challenges in tournament golf.

Playing with Byron Nelson in the first round, Demaret carried his second shot over the pond while going for the green, only to watch the ball roll back down the bank into the water. When he got to the submerged ball he had to take off his shoes and socks in order to get both feet in the water to take a stance to try to hit it out. Nor could he put his club in the water prior to making his swing because that would have been grounding the club in a hazard, an infraction of the

Demaret, top left, Byron Nelson, top right, Bobby Jones, seated left, and Ben Hogan, seated right at Augusta National. (courtesy of Historic Golf Photos)

rules. Finally he took his stance with one foot in the water and one foot on the bank, whacked at the water with his wedge, producing a cannonball-like splash, and out came the ball, coming to rest just four feet from the hole. After the magnificence of the save from the water, the birdie putt that followed seemed to be deserved. He ended that day with a 69, and then shot four under par for the next three rounds, ending with a victory margin of two strokes ahead of Nelson and Frank Stranahan.

Louise Suggs, one of the founders of the LPGA, was at the Masters that year. She and Demaret both had endorsement contracts with MacGregor and because of that she knew him. "At that time there weren't as many cars around as we have now," said Suggs, "but I had use of one that the MacGregor people had provided me. Jimmy saw me after Saturday's round and asked me if I would pick him up on my way to the golf course on Sunday. Why he didn't have a ride I cannot remember. But I did go by and pick him up. He was leading the tournament by three strokes going into the last round, and he had been tied for the lead since the first day, so I think he was feeling pretty good. While we were on our way to the golf course he said, 'Shake my hand,' and I'm sure I looked at him like he was crazy. But I shook his hand and he said immediately, 'Feel that? My fingers are thin—I'm going to win today.' And he did.

Winning the Masters in 1947 earned Demaret more attention from *Time* magazine. As usual, his attire brought notice: "He has his sports clothes made to order—in electric blue, bottle green, canary yellow, and vermilion—by a Fifth Avenue tailor. Most of all he likes to wear outlandish hats. His current favorite: a Swiss yodeler's hat. Says Jimmy: 'It keeps people talking.'" He went on to say, 'I think there is no more beautiful place in the world than a green golf course ... and I want to dress for it.'"

In the article, Demaret described the pressure of playing tournament golf: "It is the only sport where the ball is still. There is so much time for contemplation of every move you're going to make that the nerves wear thin."

Claude Harmon, the club professional who replaced Demaret at River Oaks during World War II, won the 1948 Masters. Many of the assistant professionals who worked for him at Winged Foot outside New York City over the years went on to great success in golf, including Jack Burke Jr., Mike Souchak, Dick Mayer, and Dave Marr. Sam Snead won the first of his three Masters' green jackets in 1949.

At the 1950 Masters, Demaret's attire was the subject of a story written by the Associated Press reporter covering the event. Highlights of the article included: "Dapper Demaret, on opening day, wore a stunning salmon pink sweater ... Yesterday (Friday), he wore purple pants, purple and red shoes, a knitted white golf shirt with red piping around formfitting sleeves and neckline ... When he shot 72 today (Saturday) the Blazing Blade sauntered forth in rose pants (old rose, fashion editors would call it) and a neatly matching rose and white shirt featuring a high neckline circling gracefully above a dickey ... Smiling Jimmy, who selects his wardrobe with as much care as his clubs, wore chartreuse slacks, green and white sweater, light green cap, deep green suede shoes."

In his golf to music instructional series, entitled "The Swing's the Thing," Demaret displayed the three medals awarded to him for his victories in the Masters, and he spoke of what these medals meant to him.

"They represent the proudest and most satisfying competitive victories in my career," Demaret said. "Primarily because the Masters and the Augusta National Golf Club perfectly personify everything I hold dear about golf, competitive or otherwise. The golf course and the tournament were conceived and spirited by the legendary golfer and wonderful gentleman, Bob Jones. This alone makes playing and winning the tournament an honorable thing.

"The club, the course, and the tournament have done everything possible to preserve and openly treasure the great traditions of the game as well as add to them. In the game's mad rush toward lower scores at nearly any physical price, I'm inclined to fear that many of golf's warmest and most ingratiating traditions are being ignored or forgotten. But at Augusta, during the playing of the Masters, all of these traditions are graciously, and in full measure, brought to the competition. The tournament is drenched with them. For this reason, I am proud to represent my three Masters medals as the most meaningful awards of my competitive golf life."

For the April 1960 issue of *Golf Digest,* Bobby Jones contributed an article on what he thought were the most memorable Masters tournaments up to then. Demaret's victory in 1950 was one of those singled out for special notice by Jones.

Demaret's five under par to win the tournament in 1950 did not set any records. When he finished his round of 69 on Sunday it appeared that Jim Ferrier, playing in a group behind Demaret on the course, would be the winner. Ferrier needed only a 38 on the final nine to win the tournament. He finished with a 41 coming in and

*Bobby Jones presents the winner's check to Demaret after the 1947 Masters.
(courtesy of Historic Golf Photos)*

handed the win to Demaret, who fully appreciated what had happened. After being congratulated at the closing ceremony for his victory, Demaret took the microphone and sang "Do You Know How Lucky You Are?"

Most of Demaret's performances in the Masters after 1950 were not strong enough to put him into contention. There were two exceptions. In 1957 he had no spectacular rounds, but his steady performance of 72, 70, 75, 70 gave him a third-place finish. In 1962 he managed to finish in fifth place, at that time the best finish by someone of his age, 51.

When asked about the Masters in late April of 1957, Demaret had replied, "To me the Masters is the epitome of golf, for everything it represents, the dignity, the honesty, the integrity, the class.

"The National Open is great. But the Masters is something else. In it is combined all that is great in golf. It is tough, one of the toughest, and one of the greatest challenges for the golfer."

For the April 1980 issue of *Golf Digest* Demaret was asked whether the long hitters of the era were making Augusta National obsolete. Short irons were being used to hit into the 485-yard 10th hole and the 455-yard 11th hole. Both holes have since been lengthened. "There may be a few more really long hitters today," Demaret said, "but the longest are no longer than a generation ago."

The 11th hole had been changed from the time in 1939 that Demaret first played the course, when the hole was shorter and more of a dogleg right. Demaret also recalled one of his playing partners at Augusta. "Talk about long hitters," Demaret said. "I played with Roberto de Vicenzo in 1947 and on the 13th (485 yards, par 5) he never used a driver. He hit a 3-wood around the bend and had a 7-iron for his second shot."

THE U.S. OPEN

Demaret's introduction to the U.S. Open was at Oakland Hills, outside Detroit, Michigan in 1937. He opened with a decent score of 72 on the 7,037-yard layout, but then shot 74, 76, 72 to finish tied for 16th. This was the year that Demaret's fellow Texan Ralph Guldahl won the event and he repeated as winner the next year, when Jimmy missed the cut for the tournament after shooting back-to-back 78s. He didn't play in 1938.

Then in 1939 Demaret played respectably, well enough after the first two rounds to be just three strokes behind eventual winner Byron Nelson. Demaret's 72 for the third round and then a 74 in the last round took him out of contention.

After the first round of the 1940 U.S. Open, a headline in the *Houston Chronicle* stated that "Demaret Is Seven Behind Leader," who was Sam Snead. Next to the story on the U.S. Open was a photo of Jack Burke Jr. with a caption that read: "St. Thomas College kid and son of the River Oaks Country Club pro, who enters the semifinals a favorite to win the junior Chamber of Commerce kid tournament."

The Open in 1941 was another of the events where Demaret withdrew after an unpromising start. From 1942 through 1945 the Open was canceled due to World War II, and then in 1946 Demaret managed a tie for sixth, but only a tie for 39th in 1947, though that was his best year overall on the PGA Tour.

Despite never winning the U.S. Open, Demaret in 1948 was the first golfer in U.S. Open history to break 280 when he shot 279. He still lost to Hogan, who established a new U.S. Open record at 276 when he finished several groups behind Demaret. For the time until Hogan finished after him, Demaret actually held the new U.S. Open record for total score. The rarity of shooting that low and not winning the U.S. Open is clear by noting that when Arnold Palmer lost the U.S. Open to Billy Casper in 1966, he was only the second person up to that time to have shot lower than 280 and not won the event, the other golfer being Demaret in 1948.

The 1948 event was the first time the U.S. Open was played in Los Angeles, and only the third time it had been played west of the Mississippi River. The course was set up to play 7,020 yards, at that time the longest golf course ever played for the U.S. Open.

The USGA that year was measuring the grooves on players' clubs to make sure that they met current regulations. Prior to the opening round both Demaret and Hogan had to make minor changes to their sets of clubs.

Hogan's legendary focus was evident at the Open that year. George Fazio, Hogan's playing partner, at one point holed a 4-iron shot on a par four for an eagle on the hole. At the end of the round, it was discovered that Hogan had not recorded Fazio's score as a two on the hole, and worse, it took over an hour to convince Hogan that a two was what Fazio made on the hole. Apparently, he hadn't seen the shot, didn't hear the roar of the crowd in response to the shot, nor had he seen Fazio retrieve his ball out of the hole when he got to the green.

In his book *The U.S. Open: Golf's Ultimate Challenge,* Bob Sommers described Demaret's last nine holes at the 1948 Open. "An eight-foot putt fell on the 10th, a six-footer on the 11th, and at the 12th, a 25-footer with a little too much speed slammed into the back of the cup and dropped for a third straight birdie. Two under now. A lovely long iron stopped five feet away on the 13th, a stout 440-yard par 4, but the putt hung on the lip. A stunning burst of scoring, but it won him nothing."

After an opening round 82 in the 1949 U.S. Open Demaret withdrew. His next several appearances led to finishes of T-20, T-14, T-15. Then in 1953 he put himself in contention after the Saturday morning third round of 71, only to finish with a 76 in the afternoon and come in fourth.

At the 1956 U.S. Open at Oak Hill Country Club in Rochester, New York Demaret played a round matched with Cary Middlecoff and Henry Cotton, a three-time British Open Champion. At one point when Cotton attempted to tap in a two-inch putt he missed the ball entirely, then claimed that he wasn't attempting to putt at all, but that he had been trying to right himself with his putter after losing his balance. A USGA official was summoned and asked for a ruling. After hearing the players' explanation of the situation, the official determined that he would have to accept Cotton's account of what happened. The players continued their round, but Cotton played without either Demaret or Middlecoff speaking to him again.

One of Demaret's best performances in a U.S. Open was in 1957, and it was all the more remarkable because he was 47 that year, and it was a year during which he had earlier won three PGA Tour events. The Open then required 36 holes on the final day of Saturday and though Demaret gave a valiant try when he finished with 283 and looked to be the winner, he was later overcome by both Dick Mayer and Cary Middlecoff, who finished at 282. Gene Sarazen, who had been one of the people in the clubhouse who had prematurely congratulated Demaret on winning the Open, spoke to Demaret again after Mayer and Middlecoff had finished. Demaret told him, "I wish

I had a shot at them tomorrow." Mayer beat Middlecoff by seven strokes in the play-off.

THE PGA CHAMPIONSHIP

Demaret's first appearance in The PGA Championship came in 1935, his first participation in a major. The event had been played since its beginning in 1916 in a match play format, each match featuring two players. The event was an endurance test that compares more with bicycling's Tour de France than any other golf event. Two 18-hole medal play rounds were required just to qualify for the Championship. The first three rounds were each 18-hole matches, followed by 36-hole matches for the quarterfinals, semifinals, and finals. When Johnny Revolta won The PGA Championship that year he had to prevail in 11 rounds of golf to do it, winning $1,000, and earning an average of $91 per round.

Jack Burke Sr., Demaret's friend, mentor, and former employer, failed to make it past the qualifying round in 1935, but he had seen some glory in The PGA Championship, defeating Gene Sarazen 8 and 7 in the first round of the 1925 PGA Championship, before being defeated by Harry Cooper 2 and 1 in the second round. That was just a few years after Sarazen had won the 1922 and 1923 PGA Championships and the 1922 U.S. Open. Burke had also lost in the first round of the 1928 PGA Championship to Perry Del Vecchio 1 up in a match that went to 37 holes.

Demaret lost his first round match in 1935 to Jimmy Hines, 1 down. Though not a famous player from the era, Hines played in 15 PGA Championships in his career, winning his first round matches 10 times and twice advancing as far as the semifinals.

In 1936 Demaret again did not make it past the first round, being beaten by Tony Manero 1 up, but Demaret extended the match to 23 holes before losing. In 1937 Demaret lost again in the first round, this time 2 and 1 to 1935 U.S. Open winner Sam Parks Jr.

Demaret finally advanced past the first round in the 1938 PGA Championship, defeating Frank Rodio, 5 and 4. Then he beat the

1935 PGA Champion, Johnny Revolta, 4 and 3, before losing to Gene Sarazen 1-up in a match that went to 38 holes.

The *New York Times* reported on July 13, "Any more formidable opponent than Demaret was today, Sarazen surely would have been among the missing, for his golf was anything but convincing. He took 39 to go out and was only 1 down to the Texan and wound up 1 up at noon despite a 37 on the back nine. And it was a 37 with a 2-4-3 finish, at that. Gene was 2 down until he put on that flurry.

"His golf was even worse going out in the afternoon, for he took 41, and yet lost only three holes to Demaret, who had a 38. The holes that had much to do in deciding the match were the 10th and 11th, especially the latter, which Gene won despite the fact that he had a much tougher second shot to play to the green than the Texan. An 18-foot putt on the no. 16 hole enabled Demaret to square, and a fine recovery from the rough by Sarazen on the 18th hole gave him a chance to pull out with a victory on the second extra hole." Demaret three-putted from 20 feet to give Sarazen the match.

With Demaret's remarkable performance of winning six tournaments, including the Masters, in the first half of 1940, he became one of the favorites in nearly every event he entered. He won his morning first round match against Errie Ball 3 and 2, then faced a newcomer to The PGA Championship, Eddie Kirk, in an afternoon match. Kirk, a 30-year-old golfer from Farmington, Michigan won the match in one of the biggest upsets of the event, defeating Demaret 2 and 1.

The next year Craig Wood, Masters and U.S. Open champion at age 39, was a favorite in The PGA Championship at Cherry Hills in Denver, despite having some lingering health problems. Demaret was listed as a doubtful participant just prior to the 1941 event, but he did enter and posted one of the top three scores among the qualifiers. Then Demaret lost in the first round to his former tour traveling companion, Jack Grout, 4 and 3. Wood failed in his attempt to be the first golfer to win three professional majors in one year.

In The PGA Championship in August 1942, Demaret made it as far as the semifinals, losing, 3 and 2, to Sam Snead, who went on to win the championship, defeating Jim Turnesa, 2 and 1. To make it to the semifinals, Demaret had defeated Vic Ghezzi, Tom Harmon Jr., and Craig Wood. Because of the cancellation of the event in 1943 and his service in the Navy during World War II, Demaret would not compete in another PGA Championship until 1946.

The program for the 1946 PGA Championship to be held at Portland Club in Oregon carried a half-page feature titled, "Jimmy Demaret ... Sartorially Brilliant."

"Jimmy Demaret is a newcomer to Portland who will be seen. He may be heard, too, if the day is right and he feels like singing. Demaret, for the benefit of those unacquainted with him, is easily the most colorful performer in professional golf circles these days. A great golfer, whose record is testimony enough to his accuracy with a wood or an iron, Demaret has a different outfit for every day. And to put it mildly—his sartorial getups are colorful, if not almost blinding. A Bing Crosby in reverse, he makes his living at golf and sings for fun. Uncle Sam took him from the golf scene during the war, but he's back again and the fans are happy."

Demaret first met Ben Hogan, who would defeat him soundly in a lopsided match in the 1946 PGA Championship, while playing in events around Texas in the early 1930s. Demaret later recalled in *My Partner, Ben Hogan*, that Hogan had "played in the first tournament I ever won, the Texas PGA in Dallas in 1934, and he came in about 20th." Through the 1940s the two men partnered as a four-ball team to win six PGA Tour events and eventually won two Ryder Cup foursome matches together, one for the 1947 and one for the 1951 U.S. team. When the two men met in the semifinal of the 1946 PGA Championship, Hogan did not allow friendship to get in the way of his pursuit of the title. Demaret earned a 2-up lead after the third hole, but then Hogan birdied the next three holes and at the end of the first nine he held a 3-up advantage. Hogan kept up the pace, extending his lead to 6-up by the end of the morning 18. In the afternoon round Hogan's 31 on the first nine ended the match at 10 and 9, the second biggest margin in PGA Championship match play history. Even in defeat Demaret could be affable and lighthearted. When Demaret

Demaret with Ben Hogan. (courtesy of Historic Golf Photos)

was later asked by reporters what he thought was the turning point in the match he jokingly replied, "When Hogan showed up."

The year after Demaret suffered his inglorious semifinal defeat to Hogan in Portland, The PGA Championship came to Plum Hollow Golf Club in Detroit, where he had been the club professional four years previously. In the program for the event, Ben Hogan described Demaret's enthusiasm for the event coming to Plum Hollow:

"Jimmy used to be the professional at Plum Hollow," wrote Hogan. "But he claims that is not the reason why he thinks that the gang at Plum Hollow are the most democratic bunch he has ever met.

"If you know old 'One Putt,' to use the name by which most of us tournament professionals know him, you'll know that when Jimmy likes anything or anybody he never ceases talking about it or them. Demaret has given you folks at Plum Hollow a lot to live up to. Ever since the papers were signed to stage the 1947 PGA Championship at Plum Hollow, Jimmy has been buzzing the boys about this event. 'Wait until we get to Plum Hollow' has been his war cry."

Tom Siler of the *Chicago Sun* wrote about how that year there was a "New Demaret."

"Jimmy is one of America's best golfers," said Siler, "and has been for a long time, yet frequently his wit, love of the bright lights, and prankish behavior have outshone his talent with golf sticks.

"Golfers for a long time said Jimmy could be just about as good as he wanted to be. Demaret is bearing out those predictions during the current campaign, the best of his career so far. That's why Jimmy will be one of the country's most dangerous challengers for the National PGA title at Plum Hollow.

"He has brought a new seriousness, a more mature outlook to the 1947 campaign. Jimmy admits he is slowing up on the social side and bearing down on the fairways and greens."

In an article Demaret contributed to the program for the event, he described the appeal of the club's membership, "I've never met a more democratic bunch than you'll meet right here." His reference to a "democratic bunch" was not a description of their political party. Coming soon after World War II, when democracy had to be defended, his remark was a commentary on the inclusiveness of the club. Then he went on to describe the competitive challenge of the course.

"It should be a spectator's delight," Demaret wrote. "No other course that I know of has the natural amphitheater the 18th hole at Plum Hollow provides. If that turns out to be the decisive hole for most of the matches, as it usually is at The PGA Championship, then plenty of spectators will be in on the kill. I just hope that I am not one of the ones who get murdered there.

"As you probably have been told by now, The PGA Championship is one of the toughest competitive golf tests in the world. Sizing up the course in relation to the play expected in this event I would like to predict that the golfers who par the par-3 holes consistently will win their matches.

"These par-3 holes, the second, fifth, ninth, 12th, and the 14th, are real tests. It is not unusual to have to play them with a very long iron or wood club, something that is not true of most par-3 holes at other courses."

Despite having been identified by host club pro Sam Byrd as one of the three favorites to win the event, along with Sam Snead and Ben Hogan, Demaret was eliminated in the first round by Earl Martin, 2 and 1. Yet Demaret had shot 137 in Wednesday's 36-hole qualifying round, which gave him the lowest score of all 63 qualifiers going into the match play.

The next year, at Norwood Hills Country Club in St. Louis, Demaret shot 136 in the 36-hole qualifying round, among the lowest scores. He fared better in match play this time, defeating the first Masters champion, Horton Smith, 1-up in a match that went to 20 holes. Next he defeated George Getchell 3 and 1 in an 18-hole match, Lew Worsham 3 and 1 in a 36-hole match, and George Fazio 5 and 4 in a 36-hole match. Fazio would later contribute to the design of Champions Golf Club's Jackrabbit course.

Chick Harbert accomplished what amounted to a 61 under the match play format of The PGA Championship for his match against Skip Alexander. The *New York Times* on May 23, 1948 reported "When Harbert came into the locker room after his sensational morning round Demaret asked: 'What did you have, Chick?' 'A 61,' Harbert replied as nonchalantly as he could. 'Now sit down,' quipped Demaret, 'and tell us where you missed some shots.'"

Then Demaret faced Hogan in the 36-hole semifinal, losing only 2 and 1. Both players were 10 under par when the match was closed out. Hogan went on to defeat Mike Turnesa in the final, 7 and 6, Hogan's last appearance in the event until 1960, the third year after the switch to the stroke play format. After his car accident of 1949, the 36-hole match play format of The PGA Championship, which lasted nearly an entire week, would be too taxing for Hogan's legs.

The 1949 event saw Demaret advance to the quarterfinals again with victories over Harold Oatman, George Fazio, and Jim Turnesa, before losing to eventual champion Sam Snead 4 and 3.

At Scioto Country Club in Columbus, Ohio in 1950, Demaret again advanced to the semifinals in The PGA Championship, defeating Charley Farlow, Rod Munday, and Denny Shute prior to facing Ray Gafford in the quarterfinal match. Gafford had the advantage after the first nine holes, but Demaret finished strong and won the match 5 and 4. Chandler Harper was the underdog to Demaret in the semifinal match, the third time in five years that Demaret had advanced that far. Having won his third Masters earlier that year, Demaret was definitely the favorite. But Chandler prevailed, 2 and 1, going on to win The PGA Championship 4 and 3 over Henry Williams Jr.

The book *Scioto Country Club: 75 years of History* by Paul Hornung describes the end of their match. "Demaret, clad in chartreuse slacks and singing as he walked the fairways, cut Chandler's lead to one at the 26th hole. He faced a do-or-die 15-footer on the 35th green.

"As he studied the putt, he turned to the gallery with his usual smile and remarked, 'Gracious, that hole looks small!' It was too small by an inch."

In 1951 Demaret didn't enter The PGA Championship, at the time saying, "I'm not playing in The PGA. I'm goin' fishing." Nor did he play in 1952, 1953, 1954, or 1955. The format was exhausting, requiring a 36-hole qualifier, then two rounds at 18 holes each, followed by four straight 36-hole matches. A total of 216 holes of golf in a week could be required to win the event.

The PGA eliminated the 36-hole qualifier in 1956, allowing for 128 participants, and once again Demaret participated in the match play. He won his first match over Robert Hayes quite handily, 4 and 3, but then lost to Charles Lepre 1-up in a match that went to 21 holes. Demaret was 46 years old at the time and it reinforces how competitive he was that he was still giving his best at that stage in his career.

The PGA Championship of 1956 was gratifying to Demaret for other reasons. Won that year by Jack Burke Jr., he had shown his mettle in the third round by winning 1-up in a 20-hole match with Fred Haas Jr., then in the semifinal going 37 holes to defeat Ed Furgol, 1-up. Burke defeated Ted Kroll in the final, 3 and 2, despite being 2-

down after the morning 18 holes, and losing the first hole of the afternoon round to go 3-down. Burke claimed after the round, "My chipping and putting won it for me today." Many players over the years have sought out Burke to get his assistance on their short game.

Burke had won the Masters earlier in 1956. A few years before, in 1952, Burke had won four PGA Tour events in a row, and was the last player to do so until Tiger Woods managed to win six in a row. With his achievements of the 1956 season Burke began thinking about staying closer to home, and that interest contributed to Burke and Demaret becoming interested in starting their own golf club, what would become Champions. As both Burke and Demaret had proved, they had rightfully earned the designation.

The last match play format PGA Championship was held in 1957, without Demaret participating. In his career he had participated in 13 match play PGA Championships, playing 856 holes of golf, with 22 wins out of his 35 matches, and having reached the semifinals four times, which put him on a list of only eight players who accomplished that. In the first stroke play event in 1958, Demaret opened up with a strong round of 69, which put him among the leaders, then shot a 69 in the second round. But Demaret was disqualified after the round. He had mistakenly signed his card that had a five posted for the 14th hole instead of the correct six, resulting in his disqualification. "I hate to get disqualified; I've never been disqualified in a tournament in 30 years of golf," Demaret told reporters later. "Heck, I was just making my move. I had birdied the 16th and 17th holes." This was his last appearance in a PGA Championship.

A year later, though, the program for the 1959 PGA Championship held at Minneapolis Golf Club featured a playing tip article by Demaret titled "Jimmy Demaret Demonstrates How a Texan Plays Long Irons." What he had to say about the long irons is still worthwhile advice today.

"The No. 1 iron which was referred to years ago as the 'driving iron' is virtually a nonexistent piece of equipment in the bag of the average golfer of today," Demaret said, "and the No. 2 iron is disappearing from most bags. The No. 4 and No. 5 woods have been found easier to control and handle by the less-than-expert player. Not one in 100 golfers can use these longest irons well.

"However, the No. 3 and 4 irons remain highly essential to a complete set of clubs. Inasmuch as they have less loft and a smaller striking surface than the medium and short irons, they call for an advanced degree of skill in using. Because of the limited loft on the No. 1 and 2 irons it's easy to get a smothered hook or a slice spin. I'll use a No. 4 wood every time in preference to a No. 2 iron.

"In playing the long irons I try to generate maximum club head speed, since this is the power of the long iron club.

"It is well to remember in playing the longer irons to hit through the ball and trust to the loft of the club to get the ball 'into play.' Do not try to help the ball up with the hands. This is a common fault that greatly curtails the effectiveness of the shot."

BRITISH OPEN

Demaret's one trip to the British Open had to have had part of its inspiration in Hogan's triumph at Carnoustie in 1953. Jimmy had traveled to England in 1949 for the Ryder Cup Matches, and he had played golf throughout South America, Mexico, Cuba, and Australia, so he knew that he had a game that could travel well. In his one appearance in the British Open at Royal Birkdale in England in 1954 he shot 73-71-74-71 for a respectable tie for 10th.

THE RYDER CUP

The Ryder Cup matches were not played from 1939 through 1945 due to World War II. Henry Cotton was to have captained the 1939 British Isles team. When the matches had to be canceled he sent a telegram to The PGA of America stating, "When we have settled our differences and peace reigns, we will see that our team comes across to remove the Ryder Cup from your safekeeping."

Demaret was first named to a Ryder Cup team selected for 1941 that was meant to play if somehow the war could have come to an end. That was not to be, but exhibition matches were staged between the Ryder Cup team as selected and a group of noted players, including Bobby Jones and Gene Sarazen.

David Wigner, club historian of Plum Hollow in Detroit, where one of these matches was held, has described how these matches developed.

"Walter Hagen was playing a challenge match at Inverness and bragging about how good his Ryder Cup squad would have been," said Wigner. "Gene Sarazen overheard the conversation. Sarazen was always known as a rugged individualist. He had been quite offended that The PGA left him off the 1939 squad and Hagen had not chosen him as a captain's pick. He challenged Hagen by stating that he could put together a team of 10 golfers that could beat the Ryder Cup team. Hagen accepted the challenge. Detroit Mayor Edward Jeffries and Russell Gnau, an executive with Ford Motor Company, were also at the Inverness match and were enlisted in 1940 to help put the matches together for charity. Sarazen assembled his team and lost to Hagen's Ryder Cup team 7 to 5 at Oakland Hills. The next year [1941] Sarazen talked Bobby Jones out of retirement to lead Sarazen's challengers. Gnau got the match moved to his home course, Detroit Golf Club. Jones led a major upset, as the challengers won 8 ½ to 6 ½. With the war still raging, the 1942 Ryder Cup match was held again at Oakland Hills. Hagen had not had a good year and was not chosen for the Ryder Cup team. He led the challengers but lost to Craig Wood's Ryder Cup team 10 to 5 at Oakland Hills."

Due to low attendance at the event in 1942, The PGA of America decided to find a new host site for the event in 1943. Jimmy Demaret suggested his new home course, Plum Hollow, which was selected by The PGA. Captain of the team would be Craig Wood and Jimmy Demaret, Vic Ghezzi, Lloyd Mangrum, "Jug" McSpaden, Byron Nelson, Al Watrous, Frank Walsh, and Gene Sarazen were named to the squad. Hagen (now left off the team) recruited Chick Harbert,

Members of the 1943 U.S. Ryder Cup Team at Oakland Hills Country Club. L-R: Gene Sarazen, Byron Nelson, Horton Smith, Vic Ghezzi, Captain Craig Wood, Jimmy Demaret, Ben Hogan, Ed Dudley, Harold "Jug" McSpaden, and Lloyd Mangrum. (courtesy of Plum Hollow Country Club)

Willie Goggin, Buck White, Lawson Little, Harry Cooper, Sammy Byrd, Jimmy Thomson, and Bobby Cruickshank for the challengers. The first day's matches were 18-hole four-ball.

The first day's matches were witnessed by over 6,000 spectators. "Wood paired Demaret and Ghezzi in the third match," Wigner said. "Hagen countered with his strongest team, Little and Cooper. Demaret shot 32 on his own ball on the front and they made the turn 4-up. This match was closed out on the 13th green with Demaret's team at 5-under and Little and Cooper at 1-over. Little and Cooper had taken best ball bogeys at holes 4 and 9. Because it was for charity, the players finished the 18 holes and Little had the high score of the day with a 77."

Going into Sunday's 36-hole singles matches the Ryder Cup team held a 2 ½ to 1 ½ advantage. Chick Harbert fired back-to-back 69s (they played out the holes after the match ended) to start the second day with great promise for Hagen's challengers and soundly beat Demaret 4 and 3. Demaret was 4-under par after 33 holes but it was not good enough to beat Harbert. When it was all over, the Ryder Cup team had beaten Hagen's challengers 8 ½ to 3 ½.

For the matches on Sunday more than 10,000 people attended. It was easily the best turnout of the four matches and raised over $35,000 for Red Cross relief efforts. In a war bond auction held between the morning and afternoon rounds $139,800 was raised. To raise even more money for the war effort a silent auction was held after the event. Jimmy Demaret's knitted tam o' shanter brought in $20,000, and a cowboy hat signed by all of the participants and all of the celebrities in attendance, which went for $100,000, were the two largest bids.

During 1943 this modified Ryder Cup match was the most important professional golf event. The entire PGA Tour season in 1943 consisted of only three events due to the war. The four majors had been canceled for the duration of the war. Harbert, Little, Thomson, and Ghezzi were all given leaves from active duty in the military to play in this event and help morale back home.

In 1947 conditions warranted reviving the Ryder Cup matches and Portland Golf Club in Portland, Oregon was selected as the site. Oregon businessman Robert A. Hudson funded the event by paying the expenses of the British team. In the foursomes on the first day Demaret paired with Hogan to win their match and Demaret beat Dai Rees 3 and 2 in his singles match. The American team won handily, 11 to 1.

Even for the 1949 Ryder Cup matches held in England Demaret did not tone down his attire. Charley Price wrote about Demaret's clothes: "During the 1949 Ryder cup matches in England he made an appearance in a pair of kelly green slacks, a chartreuse shirt, suede shoes in peach and purple, and argyle socks in violet and lemon, all topped off with a flapping, Dutch baker-boy cap in raspberry and turquoise plaid. The following day, just to make sure everyone knew what side he was on, he dressed in a jazz symphony of red, white, and blue that drew a salute from every member of the American team."

The U.S. team was missing Ben Hogan as a player, but he served as team captain. Byron Nelson had retired three years before and Cary Middlecoff could not participate because he was not a member of The PGA of America. Demaret paired with Clayton Heafner to win their foursomes match and then Demaret defeated Arthur Lees 7 and 6 to win his singles match, contributing to the U.S. team's victory of 7 to 5.

Demaret made the 1951 team and he and Hogan were again paired for the first day foursomes, which they won. In his singles match Demaret again faced Dai Rees, defeating him 2-up. Rees had high praise for Demaret. "Jimmy performed wondrous things in bunkers," said Rees. "I regard him as the greatest sand player I have ever seen. He was in 11 greenside bunkers that day and on 10 occasions he got down with a splash and a putt."

The match with Rees was Demaret's last as a Ryder Cup competitor, although Champions Golf Club would host the event in 1967. Demaret's playing record of six wins and no defeats is the best record for all competitors in Ryder Cup history who have played at least that many matches.

CHAPTER 5

DEMARET ON INSTRUCTION

"That Man Could Play"

◆ ◆ ◆

"Jimmy was one of those guys who would put the clubs away for a month or two and he could come right out and pick it up again," says Ben Crenshaw in describing Demaret's playing ability. "He was a player. I always remember those big hands and forearms and that sort of pigeon-toed walk of his with a big smile on his face. But the way he handled the golf club with his hands was just beautiful. He had a habit of taking the club and he would lightly twirl the club two or three times and put it down and hit the ball. It was just beautiful. And his knees and wrists were very active playing. Man alive that man could play."

Golf columnist Alex Morrison in 1953 noted how relaxed Demaret was on a golf course. "Jimmy Demaret, more than most of the players I've known, definitely shows a marked ease before and after every shot," said Morrison. "In preparing for a shot he doesn't set his jaw, lock his midsection, or go through a lot of hurried jerky movements such as taking vicious cuts at dandelions or cigar butts. His ease enables him to set up and maintain a slow tempo in going through the preliminaries before swinging at the ball."

Demaret had an appreciation that the frustrations inherent in golf, and how people handled them, revealed something about their character: "Political conventions are for the birds. If people want to determine the best presidential candidate, put all the contenders on a golf course. If a man can take five or six bogeys in a row or a succession of flubbed shots without blowing his stack, he is capable of handling any situation."

The relaxed demeanor Demaret showed on a golf course, even during the most important tournaments in which he played, did not reveal the seriousness with which he approached the game of golf. When he did discuss the game in instruction articles or in comments about the game in his various interviews he revealed that he had a great understanding of the game, that he had worked hard to develop his skills, and that his interest in playing at his best kept him focused whenever he was competing. That he contended even in major events into his 50s is an indication of how competitive he was.

After he won the Masters in 1940 and he had returned to Houston, Demaret discussed some of his concepts about the game with sportswriter Andy Anderson. More than 20 years previously Demaret

had been a caddie at Camp Logan's nine-hole golf course where Anderson worked. Fran Trimble located the articles in the old *Houston Press* and reprinted them in *Golf Houston Magazine* in April 2001.

"Personally, I know whether I will play well the instant I pick up a club," Demaret told Anderson in 1940. "The feel of the club gives me the answer. Now, if the hands are that sensitive, there must be merit in the contention the hands and forearms are the most important factors in the swing.

"It is my belief that if the hands and forearms are properly coordinated, the hips, shoulders and pivot will follow. If the hands and forearms do their work properly, timing must be correct.

"The power of a stroke generates at the feet. It passes on throughout the body to the hands; therefore, the stance is vital."

One of the foremost instructors in the game of golf in the first half of the twentieth century, Alex J. Morrison, eventually became a

The Demaret swing. (courtesy of The PGA of America)

syndicated golf columnist. Among Morrison's instructional activities was having worked with Babe Ruth on his game. Bob Hope, who lived in New York during the early 1930s while he appeared in Broadway shows, knew Morrison and later wrote about him in *Confessions of a Hooker.*

"The man who had the greatest influence on my game in the early years was Alex Morrison," wrote Hope. "He was an extraordinarily good instructor, one of the best ever. He was also a superb showman. We appeared on stage together in New York and hit those papier-mâché balls out into the audience."

Robert Joseph Allen published an article about Morrison for *Golf Magazine's Pro Pointers and Stroke Savers,* which was published in 1960. He described Morrison's development in golf: "Alex was born in Los Angeles, and got his start in golf as a caddie at the Los Angeles Country Club. Then he graduated to clubmaking under the supervision of pro Hutt Martin, a Scot from Carnoustie."

Morrison proceeded through a series of club professional jobs, and while working at the private golf course of William Wrigley at Santa Catalina Island, California he developed a theatrical routine to entertain guests vacationing there. The act was successful and led to a 25-year career in vaudeville. During this time Morrison was studying the golf swing.

"It was in 1912 that Morrison began his scientific analysis of golf," wrote Allen. "Since then his newspaper columns, magazine stories, radio programs, motion pictures, and theater exhibitions have saved strokes by the millions for golfers everywhere. His golf column for King Syndicate has been running since 1933, with a readership that is worldwide. He is also the author of one of the biggest best-sellers among sports books, *A New Way to Better Golf,* and a subsequent volume, *Good Golf without Practice.*"

Jimmy Demaret was a frequent subject of Morrison's columns. Morrison sometimes used Demaret to illustrate something about how to play the game. When Demaret won the National Celebrity Tournament in Washington in 1952, Morrison devoted a column to discussing Demaret's continuing appeal and enduring ability.

Demaret in action. (courtesy of Alex Morrison)

The Demaret follow-through. (courtesy of Alex Morrison)

"Jimmy has won from almost every champion at some time," wrote Morrison. "He has issued personal challenges for individual matches against players like Bobby Locke, yet I doubt if he is as interested in beating them as he appears. And I do believe he has an interest in the colorful side of golf that is second to none. In this department he is not excelled by any player of the past or present and my opinion includes Walter Hagen.

"And we should thank our stars that we have had a Jimmy Demaret, since golf readily becomes a mighty grim business for most players, particularly those who claim they just play for the fun of it."

In Chapter 8, titled "Hogan's Game as I See It," in the book *My Partner, Ben Hogan*, Demaret discusses his playing partner's golf skills and reveals a bit about his own concepts about the game. He starts with Hogan's grip. "If you hold the club correctly in the Hogan manner, an inverted V will be formed between the index finger and thumb of the right hand. This inverted V should point straight at your chin."

Next Demaret discusses the hitting area, claiming that Hogan had "the widest hitting area in golf," and that "He drags the club along the ground in an arc so flat that it is almost a plane." Demaret goes on to discuss "This Business of Fading," "The Simple Swing," "The Stance," "Club Selecting and Course Charting," "Putting," and "Scoring Area Shots."

A book published in 1955, *Golf with the Masters*, written by Dave Camerer, was one of the first golf instruction books that contained Demaret's insights on playing the game. The article that featured Demaret was "Playing the Punch Shot with the 5-Iron with Jimmy Demaret." The same photos of Demaret with somewhat altered text appeared in a promotional piece for a Lincoln-Mercury dealership in Ft. Worth in October 1955.

The May 1955 issue of *Golf Digest* had an article by Demaret called "Fading the Two-Iron." He begins the article by saying "Fading—or feathering—the 2-iron is a shot of considerable value, but one often overlooked by many everyday amateurs, and by some professionals, too." He might have added that few golfers could hit a 2-iron shot well enough to justify carrying the club in their bag, instead opting for a five wood. He ends the article with specific suggestions: "To summarize the 2-iron fade: 1. Grip shows only one knuckle of the left hand. 2. Line up to the left of the green. 3. Play the ball forward, with hands *over* the ball."

Thirteen years later he had another "Swing Reminder" in *Golf Digest*, this time on swaying during the swing. After explaining the fault, he makes the suggestion, "To prevent swaying, simply make sure that ample pressure is maintained on the inside portion of your right foot on your backswing. This will help you to coil, instead of sway, your body as you swing the club back."

Starting in 1959, *Golf Magazine* had a regular column from Demaret titled "The Champ's Clinic." Though Demaret was 48 years old at the time, his three wins on tour in 1957, and his three Masters wins, had sustained his credibility as an expert on the game. He answered questions about technical matters regarding the golf swing, rules questions, and he even responded when someone asked why Demaret owned more than 100 pairs of golf shoes. As was his style, Demaret could not avoid being lighthearted with some of his responses. One reader wrote that "I'm having a lot of trouble with my one-iron shots. They get out there about 235 yards and then fade about eight feet to the right. What should I do?" Demaret's helpful advice: "Turn pro."

A collection of instruction articles that had appeared in *Golf Magazine* came out in 1960, *Golf Magazine's Pro Pointers and Stroke Savers.* The last chapter included several of Demaret's Champ's Clinic responses. One reader asked: "What would be your advice to a young person who is interested in becoming a professional golfer?" Demaret's reply: "Have his head examined." In 1962, *Golf Magazine's Your Short Game* was published, a hardback anthology of instructional articles that had appeared during the magazine's first three years. The last chapter again included several of Demaret's Champ's Clinic responses on the short game.

The most complete account of everything Demaret knew about playing the game was gathered in *The Swing's the Thing,* which was produced in 1959. Charlie Crenshaw, Ben Crenshaw's father, handled some of the business matters regarding the project. The concept was unusual because Demaret had come up with the idea of teaching golf by means of a series of six 45-rpm records and eight accompanying instruction brochures. Not only were the lessons on records, he was providing background music for golfers to use as a tempo trainer for each specific shot under discussion. Dick Shannon composed and arranged the music, including a big band arrangement of a song called "The Swing's the Thing."

There was a record for putting, with a lesson on one side and practice music on the other side. There were similar records for chipping, pitching, the woods, and long irons. The best feature of the set of records may have been the introductory disc that on one side had the song "The Swing's the Thing." The recording was released in Houston as a pop record and Mercedes Demaret, wife of Jimmy's brother Mahlon, can recall driving in her car and listening to the radio when a name-that-tune contest came on with Demaret's "The Swing's the Thing" being the song to identify. The opening of the song included these lyrics:

In the office you're a peasant,
On the golf course you're a king.
With a club in hand, say you're livin' man.
The swing's the thing.

Whether you shoot in the 80s,
Or the 100s, still you'll say,
It's a lovely day on the old fairway,
The swing's the thing.

On the other side of the introductory record from the song Demaret explained how to use the series of records for instruction in the game. What he didn't explain was how someone in 1959 could have practiced their golf swing indoors standing next to the record player, or taken their record player out into the yard to be able to hear the instruction while swinging a club. Despite the instruction brochures containing as much content as any typical golf instruction book, the records must have confused golfers at the time and the set didn't sell well. Jack Treece, former superintendent at Onion Creek Golf Club in the 1970s, and a good friend of Demaret's, remembers getting a call from the widow of the man who backed the original enterprise. "Her husband had passed away and she somehow knew I would be interested in the Demaret golf to music sets, or someone gave her my name, and when she called she said she had something like 4,000 of the things all boxed up," said Treece. "This would have been in the late '70s or early '80s because Jimmy was still alive. I paid for the sets and I remember when I told Jimmy about it

The Swing's the Thing *box top.*

he gave me half of my money back that I had paid for them. I eventually sold them to a golf equipment sales representative."

Despite the unfortunate format of the information on instruction, what Demaret has to say about playing the game is valuable and

45-rpm instructional records in The Swing's the Thing *set.*

it further dispels the notion that he was a natural talent, lacking technical knowledge of the game, who did not apply himself earnestly enough to win more. For whatever reason he didn't win more there will never be an explanation, although he won enough to count among the game's top players, but it was not because he did not know what he was doing every time he stepped on a golf course.

The back of each brochure in the instruction set has a Professional Tip. Since Demaret was so well known for how he played in bad weather conditions, his comments on the wind shot are interesting.

"The ball is played off the right foot," Demaret said. "The majority of the weight is on the left foot. The hands are farther in front of the club head than they would be in the hitting of a standard short iron shot.

"The club is started low to the ground, and carried straight back, obeying the first indications of the pivot.

"But even though the natural tendencies of the pivot are being exploited by the knees, hips, and shoulders, the weight continues to stay primarily on the left foot.

"The completion of the backswing—standard in every way—except that now it becomes quite noticeable that the bulk of the weight has remained on the left foot.

THE STANCE

Jimmy Demaret

GOLF-TO-MUSIC
Lessons

(the stance)
Number 1 Fairway, Champions Golf Club, Par 4, 445 yards.

Instruction brochure in The Swing's the Thing *set.*

"Even though the majority of the weight has remained on the left foot so far, the hips and arms take the weight even farther over, to make sure the body is 'in front' of the swing pattern for this shot.

"The ball is struck hard, quickly, and the hands and arms make certain they stay in the lead well past the hitting zone. The weight is almost entirely over the left side and foot, now.

"Even at this point of the follow-through, the hands have stayed almost parallel with the ground—and insisted that the club head do so, also. The hands are very determined throughout the whole of this kind of shot.

"The highly disciplined suddenness with which this shot is struck—coupled with the tight arc caused by the resistance of the weight against the backswing's pivot—tend to end the swing at a much lower point on the follow-through."

Demaret understood that the way he could play golf was not attainable by most average golfers. He suggests in one of the professional tips in the series that a player should "Swing right and play your own game."

"There is more fun to the game if you learn to play yourself into improvement this way," he wrote, "and to do it through a kind of personal competition between what's gone before, what's happening now, and what you want to have happen in the future. Because par and regulation figures will usually chart such a nearly impossible course for you (unless you're able to devote a great deal of time to the game), you are bled of any chance for personal, satisfying achievement. Consistent par and regulation figures, in other words, are usually such lofty standards, they're almost out of the average player's reach."

CHAPTER 6

CHAMPIONS GOLF CLUB

"A Club Created by Good Players"

◆ ◆ ◆

Developing Champions Golf Club into one of the best golf clubs anywhere was definitely a collaborative effort, with many people deserving credit for the creation of the club, the success of the events the club has hosted, and the enjoyment the members have experienced during the club's history. Yet Jack Burke Jr. and Jimmy Demaret still would be acknowledged as the major contributors to the success of Champions. Their stature in the game of golf and beyond it into entertainment, politics, and business, allowed them to attract immediate interest in the club and establish its unique reputation as a haven for people who loved the game.

Asked in 1966 about the origins of Champions Golf Club for the program for the Houston Champions International Golf Tournament, Burke said, "Jimmy and I had talked about this for 15 years before we did anything about it. As a result, when we played a fine golf course we probably were a little more observant than the average players. We made mental notes of the things that appealed to us about a course, or a clubhouse, or the method of operations. So when the time came to build Champions, Jimmy and I were in almost perfect agreement on what we wanted to accomplish."

Demaret in 1950 had given an assessment of his favorite golf courses to golf writer Charley Price: "I think the best golf course I

Jack Burke in 1956. (courtesy of The PGA of America)

ever saw is Cypress Point (California). That is, for everyday play. I'll qualify that still more—it's the best 17-hole golf course I've seen. I don't care for the 18th hole there. However, for match play I think I'd have to choose Pine Valley, in New Jersey. Other great layouts are the North Course of the Los Angeles Country Club; Brook Hollow, in Dallas; the Augusta National; and Seminole, in Palm Beach, Florida."

Demaret and Burke had played on the best competition courses in the world, and they had won on them. Now they were interested in creating a club that would have those features that they had appreciated elsewhere. Once the project was underway, Demaret was so involved he even drove earthmoving equipment while the land was being cleared of trees. Jack Burke recalled the process for the club's first history: "Jimmy had a lot more to do with building the club than I did," said Burke, "but I'd get home [from the PGA Tour] as often as I could and we'd spend all of our time at the property. Jimmy and I hit hundreds of golf shots on the various holes to get a better idea how to build them. And Ralph Plummer was great. He welcomed our help, and the three of us worked together well as a team."

Ralph Plummer is credited as the architect for Cypress Creek, the first course at Champions Golf Club. He and Demaret had worked together with John Bredemus in building Hermann Park and Memorial Park 30 years before the Champions project began. Among Plummer's many designs across the country was Shady Oaks in Ft. Worth, Ben Hogan's home course, which gave Plummer credibility with Demaret and Burke.

In a preview in *Golf Digest* of the television show *All-Star Golf* for the 1960 season, Champions, which was going to be one of the sites for the show's matches that year, was featured. "Golfers who stray from the rather wide fairways could often use a compass," said the article. "There is at least a 50-yard width of wooded area between each fairway.

"Two streams meander through the course and help provide interesting water hazards. The 246-yard, par-3 fourth is one hole in which the stream plays an especially important part. The green is behind a bank of the creek and in order to hit the putting surface from the back tee a golfer must fly his shot about 200 yards.

"All of the par-4s require good shots in order to negotiate them in standard figures. One of the most challenging of these is the 17th, which hovers on the left of the fairway for the last quarter of the distance to the green, a forbidding hazard for hookers."

The name for the club had been suggested by Jack Valenti, who during the 1960s spent several years as a political advisor to Lyndon Johnson when he was president. Valenti has served as president of the Motion Picture Association of America for many years. In the late 1950s Valenti was working in marketing in Houston in a firm he had founded with Weldon Weekley. They got involved with the new golf course development project devised by Burke and Demaret. Valenti set about finding a name for the new club. Seizing on the obvious, but also the ingenious, Valenti suggested that they call the club Champions in respect for all of Demaret's and Burke's accomplishments. Everyone involved liked the name, and after convincing Demaret and Burke, that is what it became. That the club has hosted a Ryder Cup, a U.S. Open, the Southern Amateur, and various other significant tournaments further confirms that it was appropriately named.

While the firm of Weekley and Valenti contributed the name for the club and assisted with the marketing campaign to attract members to the club, there were several other businessmen who assisted Demaret and Burke with the more mundane aspects that made the venture a success. In the early stages of the development of Champions, Horace Norman was credited with being an invaluable contributor to the business needs of the club's growth. By 1959 Pat Morgan had become involved to develop the real estate around the club and he made significant contributions. As the club began operations Bob Hogan (no relation to Ben Hogan) and Dr. Les Lemak influenced the club, ensuring competent management in every area.

The Cypress Course at Champions opened for play on November 1, 1958. At that time the clubhouse was still under construction,

Champions Golf Club clubhouse. (courtesy of The PGA of America)

but by the spring of 1959, that was ready and the Grand Opening took place on April 21, 1959. Grand it was with a guest list that included Bing Crosby, Ben Hogan, Mickey Mantle, Randolph Scott, James Garner, and Mike Souchak, among other celebrities. More than 6,000 spectators turned out for the event. Later in the year the club named its first head professional, Jimmy Burke, Jack's brother, who was later tragically killed in a car accident not far from Champions. Tad Weeks has been the head professional at the club for over 20 years. Shirley Sembritzky, now the club's manager, has had a long tenure with the club, and several other staff members are long-term employees.

With the success of the club there began a need for a second 18, and for that course George Fazio was brought in to do the golf course design. Demaret and Burke had competed against Fazio when he was active on the PGA Tour from the late 1940s into the 1950s. Because they wanted a different look for their second course it was decided that they needed a different golf course architect. The second course was named Jackrabbit and it opened in July of 1964 for the members, with the official festivities in April of 1965. During 2001 and 2002 the Jackrabbit Course was renovated by George Fazio's nephew, Tom Fazio.

Less than 20 years after the club was started, it merited a club history written by Bob Rule and published in 1976. Ben Hogan wrote a foreword for the book, in which he recognized Demaret and Burke for their achievement with Champions.

"Jimmy and Jackie have been close personal friends of mine for a great many years, and when they started the club 20 years ago I knew they had many things in their favor," Hogan wrote. "Their knowledge of the things club members and professionals alike would want and need in a golf club, plus the very way the two men think, made you believe their club couldn't be anything but successful."

Hogan also credited Burke and Demaret for the success of the events hosted by the club. "The Ryder Cup Matches at Champions in 1967 were well planned and carried out. Everything about the event reflected the style and class of Burke and Demaret—the dinners before and after the event, the impressive opening ceremonies, and the many niceties the players enjoyed. Jimmy and Jackie were the 'why' things were done properly.

"They also were hosts in 1969 to the U.S. Open Championship, and again the club did a fine job of handling the many arrangements and caring for the needs of the players."

Earl Elliott was one of the key people in directing many of the events over the years at Champions. For the U.S. Open in 1969 held at Champions Elliott was cochairman along with Jack Burke for the local tournament committee. At that time, Elliott was president of the Houston Golf Association. Elliott, who contributed to golf in Houston in many ways, had a scholarship in his name funded at Rice University in appreciation for his support of golf. Jack Burke Jr. was one of the key people who established the Earl Elliott Humanities Scholarship Fund at Rice in 2002. Also contributing were Champions Golf Club, the Houston Golf Association, and the PGA Tour, Inc.

Jack Burke Jr.

Eddie Merrins, the head professional at Bel Air Country Club in Los Angeles from 1962 until 2002, described the appeal of Champions Golf Club for the better players. "Jack Burke and Jimmy Demaret established a camaraderie at Champions," said Merrins, "especially among the better players, who felt very welcome at the club. At one time the club had five different PGA Championship winners among its members, including Jack Burke, Dave Marr, Jay Hebert, Lionel Hebert, and John Mahaffey. Steve Elkington among contemporary players is a member. I believe that they have always been diligent about who they allowed into the club in terms of playing ability. It's a club created by good players, which is a rarity among golf clubs, and it may be unique in that way."

Merrins thinks the ability of Champions Golf Club to attract the Ryder Cup and the U.S. Open less than 10 years from the opening of the club relates to the way the club has always been managed.

"There are no committees at Champions," Merrins continued, "which at many clubs can complicate the process of considering whether to host an event. At Champions, Jimmy and Jack made up their minds to host events and that was that. At most clubs it takes an act of Congress to get something approved. The other factor about why Champions attracted these events is that Jimmy and Jack were prominent members of the golf world, everyone knew them and liked them, and everyone appreciated that they had created something special at Champions. The club had a lot of attention from the time it opened."

Merrins played college golf at LSU from 1952 to 1955. At that time college athletes had three years of eligibility. He originally intended to remain an amateur player, but in 1957 he learned of a job opportunity at Merion in Philadelphia and started his career as a club professional there. He moved on to Rockaway Hunting Club in Cedarhurst, the oldest club in the New York metropolitan area, and also taught with Claude Harmon at Thunderbird. On October 1, 1962, he came to Bel Air in Los Angeles where he has worked since that time.

During his years as a club professional Merrins played in more than 200 PGA Tour events, which is how he became acquainted with Jack Burke and his brother Jimmy, as well as Jimmy Demaret. When Merrins played in his first U.S. Open in 1957, he recalls being paired with Don Cherry and Rex Baxter, two amateurs. Their group was playing behind the group that included Hogan, and behind Merrins's group was the group that included Demaret. Two of the most famous players on tour for the past 20 years were ahead of them and behind them. Merrins described his group as a "hot dog" pairing. When people would look at who was following Hogan, and seeing that Demaret was following Merrins's group, they would turn to their fellow spectator and say, "Let's go get a hot dog."

On an evening prior to the first round of the 1957 U.S. Open, Merrins was in the bar of the hotel where he was staying. He found himself situated between Tommy Bolt and Walter Hagen, who immediately proceeded to interrogate Merrins about why he had made the mistake of becoming a golf professional. "No matter what I would have told them that night," said Merrins, "they were determined to verbally flip me up in the air a couple of times."

Merrins was at Champions in October of 1999 for the PGA Tour Championship, which followed the tragic plane crash that included Payne Stewart. The plane's ultimate destination was Houston, after a stop scheduled in Dallas for a golf course site inspection. A memorial service for Stewart became part of the program at the PGA Tour Championship.

"There was a mist fog covering the course that day," said Merrins. "For the beginning of the ceremony a single bagpiper made his way from out of that fog toward the group assembled for the ceremony. You could hear the playing before you could even see the bagpiper. Once he did appear, in plus fours, his attire was such an instant reminder of Payne Stewart that it almost seemed to be an apparition."

As though Jack Burke could always summon up the appropriate elements for an event, a similar occurrence for the 1967 Ryder Cup ceremony added some drama to the activities. Houston professional Dick Forester recalled the ceremonies for that Ryder Cup for an article by David R. Holland for golftexas.com.

"One of the most stirring things I've ever seen in golf happened at the Ryder Cup at Champions in 1967," Forester remembered. "You always have an opening ceremony where they play both American and British national anthems. Well, we had a fog delay, and out of that fog appears 200 University of Houston marching band members playing 'The Star-Spangled Banner.' I'll never forget that."

Forester, like Demaret, had been a caddie as a boy. "Back then there was no competition like there is today. We just watched the good players and tried to imitate them. Today you have coaches and videos and everything is so organized. And the courses are in such good condition." Demaret brought Forester down from Michigan to work as an assistant professional at River Oaks Country Club, where Demaret had first worked as a teenager, and then later worked as a pro himself. Forester became head professional at River Oaks after Demaret left in 1945. Then Forester went on to be head professional at Houston Country Club for more than 20 years, then worked at Bear Creek Golf World for the remainder of his career.

Forester and Demaret were present for the founding of the Houston Golf Association in 1945. A group of Houstonians wanted a PGA Tour event for the city, and the Houston Golf Association was formed to provide volunteers to assist in running the tournament, which was first staged in 1946 and won by Byron Nelson.

Forester was a key figure in Texas golf throughout his career and at the national level of the game. He became a member of The PGA of America in 1942 and later served on the organization's executive committee. He helped attract the Ryder Cup to Houston, as well as the Texas State Open. Prior to the opening of Champions for play, Forester witnessed what Jimmy Demaret claimed was a hole-in-one on a par-3 hole.

"Demaret hit this shot on the green and declared he had the first hole-in-one recorded at Champions," Forester recalled. "I said, 'wait a minute, there aren't any holes or flags out there yet.' He said: 'Well, if there were holes that would be the spot, so I made a hole-in-one.'"

An amateur event was inaugurated in 1961 at the club called the Champions Cup Matches, which had 70 two-man teams. Some of the nation's leading amateur players of the time competed in the matches, including Deane Beman, Charley Coe, and E. Harvie Ward. One of the players in those early Champions Cup matches was Charlie Crenshaw, father of Ben Crenshaw, winner of the 1984 and 1995 Masters. Ben knew Jimmy Demaret from the time Ben was a child.

"My father, when he got out of Baylor Law School, went to Houston to live and he worked in the attorney general's office in Houston," said Crenshaw. "He met Jimmy Demaret way back in Houston. That's in the early '40s, before the war. They just started seeing each other a little more and my dad played in various tournaments. My father went to the Odessa Pro-Am in West Texas where Jimmy also played. He would see Jimmy Demaret there. When Champions Golf Club was started they instituted the Champions Cup matches and my father was on some of the first teams there from Austin with

Jimmie Connolly, who later partnered with Jimmy in developing On- ion Creek. When they were developing Onion Creek my father and Jimmy were on assignment to secure the water rights necessary for the golf course.

"Another venture of Jimmy's that my father was involved in was those little golf to music lessons that Jimmy came up with, *The Swing's the Thing*, right around the start of Champions. Actually my father did the legal work on that.

"The first time I met Jimmy, I think I was about 10 years old, in 1962, and he came to open up a driving range in south Austin for one of his friends. It was in the evening and he came and did an exhibi- tion, and that was my first time to meet Jimmy Demaret. And also right around that same time, though, my father took me to my first professional golf event down in San Antonio at Oak Hills, the Texas Open. That was I think in about 1963 or '62 and we saw Jimmy and some other players out on the course that day. He came over and talked to my brother and me and my dad. We had a great time. He was always really, really kind to us as little kids. Then a few times I would accompany my dad down to Champions for the Champions Cup matches, and I got to see Demaret a little bit more. Then I saw him some when I spent time out at Onion Creek. There just never was a more infectious personality than Jimmy Demaret. He was the funniest guy. Everybody loved him. He was a modern day Walter Hagen, really.

"Some of my other memories of Jimmy include when I was asked one day to compete on a television show that featured Arnold Palmer—the best 18 holes in America, chosen by Arnold. The 14th hole at Champions was picked for one of the holes. I went down one day and Arnold and I played the 14th hole and Jimmy Demaret was the commentator. That was in 1972, I think. Then we played the Southern Amateur there in 1973. I won that—that was wonderful to win a nice tournament like that at Champions. I also played at Cham- pions when they hosted the Houston Champions International in 1971 and finished seventh in the tournament.

"When I turned professional Jack Burke said I just want you to remember something. He said, the first three letters in the word professional is p-r-o, but that should not be professional to you, it should be promote. That means you should promote the game wherever you can.

"Several years after Jimmy passed away, Onion Creek decided to add 9 holes. They had adjacent property available and Bill Coore and I added 9 holes there, but Jimmy had a great eye for architecture in the work he did on the original 18 holes at Onion Creek. He learned from a fellow named John Bredemus, who was pretty instrumental in early Texas golf. Jimmy was a good architect and he learned to enjoy building courses for John. Jimmy did a very interesting thing that Jimmy Connolly told me. When he wanted to build a bunker, Jimmy would look at a location for a bunker, either an artificial mound or a place he thought a bunker might look good and he would get a rope like a lasso and he would put it on the ground in any shape he wanted. And he would look at it and go back and look at it a little bit and say that's good and sometimes he would change the rope around. That's a pretty good way to do it. Simple."

Crenshaw and his partner Bill Coore have won considerable recognition for their golf course design work. Sand Hills in Nebraska is recognized as one of the best designs done in the past 40 years. Crenshaw expressed great respect for what was accomplished at Champions.

"Cypress Creek at Champions is a golf course that has really stood the test of time," said Crenshaw. "Wonderful golf course. I think some of the guys that go back there each two years for the Tour Championship, they really enjoy playing that course and it is a very modern course. It's still one of the spots where even all the long hitters hit drivers and that's pretty rare these days. Jimmy and Jackie kept up with the times and it was always a great test of golf. With the wider fairways and big greens you can set up Cypress Creek a lot of different ways. Very different, especially if you maintained it firm and fast and put in some interesting flagstick locations. It's a wonderful test of golf."

"I think it's really neat when I go back to the Masters every year," said Crenshaw, "I share a locker with Jimmy in the Champion's Locker Room."

Don Cherry was another participant in the early Champions Cup matches. Cherry had met Demaret when both participated in the Masters in the 1950s, and both shared a love of singing. Cherry was an amateur golfer through the '50s, including having a 5-0 record in Walker Cup play on three teams and he won 14 amateur titles. While still an amateur he came close to winning the U.S. Open at Cherry Hills in 1960 before finishing in seventh.

Demaret admired Cherry's singing, and the public loved him. Cherry had a number one hit with "Band of Gold" and successes with "Take a Message to Mary" and "Wild Cherry." In a profile of Cherry in the January 2003 *Links* magazine, he told writer Tom Chiarella about Demaret: "Jimmy was what my father should have been. He really took care of me." They were great friends, but that didn't stop Demaret from his usual practical jokes and other nonsense. In one incident, Demaret smuggled a foghorn into a nightclub where Cherry was performing. Just as Cherry began to truly connect with the crowd, Demaret let go a blast from the foghorn. Not one to give up on a good thing, Demaret called Cherry at his hotel room later, supposedly to apologize for the earlier prank, only to let out another rip from the foghorn.

Cherry turned professional in 1962, but Demaret, who was unaware of the change in Cherry's status, sent Cherry an invitation to participate in the Champion's Cup. Cherry wrote back that he could not participate because he was now a professional. Not one to miss an opportunity, Demaret wrote back: "Dear Don, to me you'll always be an amateur."

Charlie Wilson was one of the first members of Champions Golf Club and one of the first of the homeowners in the neighborhood. He had become friends with Burke first and then through him met Demaret. Because he was a professional pilot and Jimmy was becoming more interested in flying in the 1950s they spent a lot of time together. Wilson recalls their first visits to Austin to scout out the

Demaret's friend Charlie Wilson when he was a young pilot. (courtesy of Charlie Wilson)

site for Onion Creek Golf Club. On some trips to visit the property they would land where the property had been cleared for the fairways of the golf course. Demaret was frequently at the Wilson house and when Wilson's two boys, Cary and Curtis, were old enough, Demaret would sometimes take one or the other of them with him flying. Curtis later became a pilot for Federal Express.

"I met Jackie Burke before I met Jimmy," said Wilson. "I was flying for the Philippine Airline after World War II. I joined a golf club called WacWac in Manila, named after a bird that roosted around there and said WacWac. I read where they were going to have the Philippine World Open. Leading players coming from all over. The four that came from the U.S. were Jackie Burke, Lloyd Mangrum, Porky Oliver, and Joe Kirkwood Jr. After the four day tournament, Mangrum won it, Burke was second, Porky was third. That was my first introduction to golf pros. I flew them out there to Wake Island. Lloyd Mangrum had just won the U.S. Open in 1946. So Jackie says if you ever come back to the States, call me. So we corresponded a few times. I sent him some stuff. So sure enough, I had a chance for a job offer in Houston in 1956. So I called Jackie and said would you call up this fellow and you tell him I'd like a job. So through Jackie's help, I got the job in Houston. Of course, right off I meet Burke's friend, Jimmy Demaret. I bought a house not far from Jack. Once they started Champions, I joined the club and bought a house in the neighborhood. Eventually, it got to be that Jimmy would come over nearly every day.

"One time we went to Palm Springs, we went to Bermuda a couple of times, we went to Mexico many times fishing. We would go to the Concord Hotel in New York. We went to South Texas on fishing trips and out to Jimmy's ranch to go hunting. We flew down to Miami for the Super Bowl one year. We got to all four corners of North America. Jimmy bought a Beechcraft Debonair airplane in 1963. He was always thinking of some place to go, and he was always asked to go someplace. He was quite popular. We had dinner one night with Frank Sinatra in Palm Springs, California because we knew two guys who worked for Sinatra who knew Ken Venturi, and Jimmy knew Venturi. We spent time with Bob Hope."

After Jimmy died in 1983, Wilson decided to honor him by having a bust sculpted that could be displayed at Onion Creek Golf Club in Austin, the site of the first Legends of Golf tournament.

"The bust of Jimmy I had presented to Onion Creek was done by a former pilot in World War II, Harold Graham, and he sculpted for the fun of it; he didn't sell his work. He had never seen Jimmy Demaret. So I took him the few snapshots I had. From snapshots he did a sculpture. The sculpture is sitting in front of Onion Creek Golf Club at the pro shop. Golfers can see Old Jimmy smiling at them.

"Jimmy never forgot someone's name, no matter where he met somebody. One time, Jimmy and I checked into a hotel in downtown New York City. We got a cab from the airport. We checked into the hotel, went and had a couple of drinks and went to bed because it was late. The next morning he was waking me up—let's go. It isn't even light outside. Well, he says, I've got to go take a walk. We go down, and he said, I tell you where there's a good place to get breakfast. A yellow cab pulls up to the front of the hotel. And he says. Hey, cabbie. How the hell are you, buddy. This cab driver had carried him years before. Jimmy says. How are you doing? How's Myrtle? How are the kids? I didn't know what the hell—here we are in New York City. But he remembered him. Of course, the cab driver didn't charge us to go 4 or 5 blocks. But Jimmy was fabulous with names. I wondered: How in the hell could he remember this? It was as if it was 30 minutes ago."

Demaret frequently created nicknames for his friends. Charlie Wilson became 'Hong Kong' Wilson.

"Oh, how I got the name Hong Kong. Jimmy would always help the caddies out. He'd let a caddie walk alongside our cart. Stuff like that. He just did it to give them 10 dollars. So there was a caddie named 'Blackbird' out at Champions. One day, Jimmy and I are talking on the golf cart and we're talking about where we'd been and I'd been. I said, there is one place I'd like to go back and that's to Hong Kong because it was a fabulous city. The next time I went over to Champions, there was Jimmy and he was waiting on me to play golf. And Blackbird. So Blackbird said: Hi, there, Hong Kong. I think

Jimmy put him up for that. Jimmy had a nickname for everybody. Charles Newman became Chilly. So Hong Kong stuck on me. Other people began to call me that and my name got to be Hong Kong. One night in 1968 at Champions, I got a postcard from Jimmy, who was in the Far East and the postcard says, 'Hong Kong, why don't you try to meet me in Manila? Cheers, Jim.' He was going to be there for a segment of *Shell's Wonderful World of Golf.* I did meet him that trip. We did a week together. I got to show him my old golf club.

"Every Christmas Day he would come by our house. In the trunk of his car, whatever he was driving—a Lincoln or a Cadillac—he always had plenty of bottles of booze: bourbon and rum and scotch and gin. And there would always be a bunch of caddies around the caddie yard at the Champions. He had already been by Memorial and Hermann Park and maybe one other on the way to Champions. Most of the booze was gone by that time. But he'd go up there and open the trunk and give them all a bottle of booze on Christmas. I always thought that was a nice little gesture."

Champions was successful from the start. The list of the honorary members has included Bob Hope, Bing Crosby, Perry Como, James Garner, Randolph Scott, Ed Sullivan, Ben Hogan, Mickey Mantle, Mike Souchak, and astronauts Admiral Alan Shepard and Lt. Colonel Charles Duke. Another honorary member, Gene Cernan, the last American to walk on the moon, became a member at Champions during the 1960s, and he would become one of Jimmy Demaret's closest friends for the rest of his life. Cernan moved to Houston in January of 1964 to be an astronaut.

Born in Chicago in 1934, Cernan described his relationship to Demaret as "between a father and a brother." They met when Cernan was invited to play golf at Champions. Demaret would later tell him, "Gene, you hit your woods well; you're just having trouble getting out of them." Meeting Demaret, Cernan said "he acted like he had been waiting to meet you all day long."

In terms of formal education, the two men could not have been more different. Demaret did not complete high school. Cernan received a bachelor of science degree in electrical engineering from

Purdue University in 1956 and a master of science degree in aeronautical engineering from the U.S. Naval Postgraduate School, Monterey, California. However, both men were pilots, they both enjoyed the outdoors and golf, they both had been inducted into several halls of fame for their accomplishments, and they shared a mutual respect.

Cernan's accomplishments deserve a detailed review. He was one of 14 astronauts selected by NASA in October 1963. He occupied the pilot seat alongside command pilot Tom Stafford on the Gemini IX mission in June of 1966. During this three-day flight, Cernan, the second American to walk in space, logged two hours and ten minutes outside the spacecraft in extravehicular activities.

On his second space flight he was lunar module pilot of Apollo 10, May 18–26, 1969, the first comprehensive lunar-orbital flight test of an Apollo lunar module. He was accompanied on the 248,000 nautical mile sojourn to the moon by Thomas P. Stafford (spacecraft commander) and John W. Young (commander module pilot).

Cernan made his third space flight as spacecraft commander of Apollo 17, the last scheduled manned mission to the moon for the United States, which commenced on December 6, 1972, and concluded on December 19, 1972. With him on the voyage of the command module "America" and the lunar module "Challenger" were Ronald Evans (command module pilot) and Harrison H. (Jack) Schmitt (lunar module pilot). While Cernan and Schmitt conducted activities on the lunar surface, Evans remained in lunar orbit aboard the "America" completing various tasks.

In September 1973, Cernan assumed additional duties as Special Assistant to the Program Manager of the Apollo Spacecraft Program at the Johnson Space Center. On July 1, 1976, Captain Cernan retired after over 20 years with the U.S. Navy. He concurrently terminated his formal association with NASA.

Cernan was the second American to have walked in space. He was one of the two men to have flown to the moon on two occasions, and as commander of the last mission to the moon, Apollo 17, had the privilege and distinction of being the last man to have left his footprints on the surface of the moon.

Demaret at the controls of his Beechcraft B33 Debonair in September of 1963.
(*courtesy of* Golf Digest)

His honors include being awarded two NASA Distinguished Service Medals, the NASA Exceptional Service Medal, the JSC Superior Achievement Award, two Navy Distinguished Service Medals, the Navy Astronaut Wings, the Navy Distinguished Flying Cross, the Federation Aeronautique Internationale Gold Space Medal for 1972, and induction into the U.S. Space Hall of Fame.

Prior to meeting Jimmy Demaret in the mid 1960s, Cernan was looking forward to it because, he said, he would be meeting "a real celebrity."

Cernan described the qualities that made Demaret a good pilot. "What makes a good pilot—you've got to think ahead, understand where you are and what you're doing. Demaret did all the right things, knew the rules, knew his airplane. If you're going to be a pilot, you've got to be a professional. Jimmy understood the significance of weather. He didn't take unnecessary risks. He was serious about flying, maybe in some ways the same as he approached golf. Then again, he had such strong arms and hands. He was very securely attached to the controls and very sure in his handling of the plane."

Demaret had a ranch near Van Horn, Texas that he had bought with a few friends. Cernan would visit there and occasionally go hunting with Demaret, sometimes late at night for "varmits," rabbits and other small animals that might be prowling around. On one trip to another friend's ranch, Cernan and Demaret went out turkey hunting. They came upon a turkey, 100 yards away. Demaret had his 22 rifle pointed 30° up, away from the ground, and he pulled the trigger. Two seconds later the turkey fell over dead. Cernan is still convinced that the turkey had a heart attack. "Jimmy loved to go hunting because it was outdoors and he was with people. He wasn't a trophy hunter, and most of the time I think he was aiming away from whatever he was supposed to be shooting."

Golf writer Charley Price related a similar story about Demaret in 1950: "An irate guide who had spent days tracking down deer for Demaret caught him shooting straight up in the air at a retreating buck which originally had been only a few yards from him." Bing Crosby at the time said of Demaret: "I believe he honestly thinks he is taking advantage of wild game when he hunts them. He feels he ought to give them one up."

In later years, Demaret had a ranch west of Houston where Cernan kept his horses. He would take his daughter out to Demaret's ranch to ride. Cernan also recalled flying a helicopter out to Champions, with Demaret coming outside to act as a flagman for the landing on the driving range.

Demaret first learned to fly in late 1939. Charlie Walling, the man who gave Demaret his first flying lessons, later recalled Demaret coming to Houston Municipal Airport and asking "What does it take to learn how to fly?" At the time lessons were $7 an hour, and usually it took eight hours of flight time before a pilot could learn to solo. A physical was required at the time prior to a pilot getting authorized to solo and for some reason, which Walling never learned, Demaret would not get the physical, so he did not solo at the time. In the 1950s he fully completed the physical and passed his solo requirements.

When he was first learning to fly Demaret would go out to the airport late in the day, sometimes bringing his golf clubs and hitting balls near the office where Walling worked. They maintained their relationship through the years, although during Demaret's most active period of travel from the early 1940s into the early 1950s, they rarely saw each other. When Champions opened, Walling began playing golf with Demaret at the club.

Demaret decided in 1961 to buy a DC-3 plane, assisted by a few other investors, with the idea of flying groups of primarily Champions Golf Club members to various sports events or fishing trips. Walling served as the pilot. The idea appealed for about a year, and then after interest faded the plane was sold.

Some sense of the impact of Champions Golf Club and its surrounding home community on northwest Houston is evident in the growth of land values. When Champions was being developed land in the area could be purchased for $600 an acre. Eventually the land in the area would become worth more than $200,000 an acre. The club's stature in the world of golf has only grown, with significant tournaments hosted there regularly, such as the 2003 PGA Tour Championship.

CHAPTER 7

DEMARET THE ENTREPRENEUR

"The Greatest Slacks I've Ever Worn"

◆ ◆ ◆

During the time Demaret was most active on the PGA Tour, from 1938 through 1958, there were other players who won more events than he did, including Sam Snead, Byron Nelson, Ben Hogan, Lloyd Mangrum, and Cary Middlecoff. But none of them had Demaret's appeal as a personality. He was able to translate his appeal into product endorsements, broadcast announcing, and other business opportunities. In a sense even the opportunity to develop Champions Golf Club reflected the appeal of Demaret and Burke in Houston, and the respect they had earned from their fellow businessmen.

Even before he had won a PGA tour event Demaret had managed to attract the attention of an equipment manufacturer wanting to benefit from the appeal of his personality to sell products. The June 1956 *Golf Digest* cover story on him describes his introduction to product endorsements. "It all started back in 1937, when Demaret was a gregarious 27-year-old youth who had yet to seriously dent the prize purses. Golf equipment manufacturing companies had not gotten into the habit of signing big-name pros to their advisory staffs — for a fee. But Jimmy fixed that.

"Invited to perform on bandleader Sammy Kaye's radio program, the ex-caddie from the plains of Texas gave out with such melodious songs and nimble humor that he was an immediate hit. One of the men he intrigued was Toney Penna, then and now an official in the MacGregor Golf Company. Penna signed Demaret to represent his company, and the association has lasted to this day."

Penna himself wrote about how Demaret came to be affiliated with MacGregor in the book *My Wonderful World of Golf* that appeared in 1965. "The first player I thought of signing up for MacGregor was Jimmy Demaret," wrote Penna. "Jimmy was one of the finest, brightest, most colorful personalities in the game, and still is. I knew that he was a fine player who was going to make a lasting mark on the game."

To get Demaret on the MacGregor payroll, Penna had to convince his boss, a Mr. Rickey, that a 27-year-old golfer from Texas who had yet to win on the PGA Tour would make a major contribution to the MacGregor company's sales. The compensation from golf equipment companies in that era was modest. "In those early days we would sign a good player for $500 and the company would match the purse they earned in winning one of the major tournaments," as Penna described the benefits.

Mr. Rickey disagreed about Demaret's potential, so Penna arranged for Demaret to join him and Mr. Rickey for dinner during the week of the U.S. Open. They went to a night spot where the orchestra of Wayne King was playing. King, who knew Jimmy, "asked Demaret, with quite a vocal buildup, to come to the bandstand and sing a number with him." Mr. Rickey was impressed.

"Toney," Mr. Rickey said, "I don't know whether this boy can play golf or not, that's your department, but as far as a goodwill ambassador is concerned, sign him up because he's worth every penny of it. He sure has what it takes and all the personality that I'm looking for, because I think that's just as important in selling golf clubs as it is to be able to play with them."

Penna himself had the opportunity soon thereafter to be signed to an endorsement contract with a toothpaste company. The company's representative asked Demaret's opinion.

A page from a sporting goods catalog in 1940.

"You'd better be careful about this guy," Jimmy said with a straight face. "He has teeth but he washes them with Sani-Flush."

Penna was victimized by Demaret in a more dramatic way when they were traveling with Tommy LoPresti, another PGA Tour professional.

"On this particular afternoon I had just taken a bath when there was a knock on the door," Penna remembered. "I had a towel in my hand and I held it draped loosely around me while I cautiously opened the door and peered out. There stood Demaret."

"Why don't you just come on in?" Penna asked him.

"No sooner were the words out of my mouth than LoPresti, who had stolen up beside me by coming through the connecting door [between our rooms], snatched the towel and before I knew it had pushed me out into the hall and slammed my door and locked it. Demaret meanwhile had dashed down to the door to the connecting room and slammed the door behind him. There stood Penna stark naked in the hall, right in front of where the elevators were busily going up and down."

After a brief episode when Penna was forced to use a mop to shield his modesty from three ladies coming down the hall, he was rescued by a house detective who was called by another hotel guest.

The MacGregor Golfsmith sports equipment catalog for 1950 displayed the Jimmy Demaret signature Pacemaker woods and irons. The catalog described the merits of the woods: "The Jimmy Demaret Pacemaker model, fundamentally designed for the less accomplished golfer, has many quality features to help these players get the correct 'feel' of the game. This head model offers a larger hitting area to help the less accurate swinger."

The catalog copy for the Jimmy Demaret Pacemaker Clubs had been a little different 10 years previously: "The feel is there, you can't miss it. The fine grip, the powerful shaft, the head, its colors and depth of face. Here we offer a club worth carrying in any golf bag. Enjoy the swing and feeling of a clean hit shot with this club." In 1940 the clubs sold for $3.26 each for a driver, brassie, or spoon, all woods. In the 1950s Demaret promoted a putter that MacGregor made that featured a slot in the top of the grip for four metal discs—ball markers.

During the 1940s, Demaret made several appearances on national radio programs. When the television era began in the late 1940s and

Demaret with Cary Middlecoff, Glenn Ford, and Ben Hogan during the filming of Follow the Sun. *(courtesy of The PGA of America)*

early 1950s, he first made guest appearances, as well as playing a cameo role in a film.

The film biography of Ben Hogan's life, *Follow the Sun,* premiered on March 23, 1951 in Ft. Worth, Texas. The story covers Hogan's life up through his losing effort against Sam Snead in a play-off for the 1950 Los Angeles Open, about one year after his car accident. Jimmy Demaret played himself in a couple of scenes. Dennis O'Keefe played a character called Chuck Williams based very loosely on Demaret, or as is said in the film business, a composite. O'Keefe plays a wise-cracking, happy at all times, friend of Hogan. In the movie the O'Keefe character tries to make Hogan, played by Glenn Ford, feel guilty that he is winning so many tournaments and making things tough for everybody else, including the 10 and 9 beating Hogan gave Demaret in the 1946 PGA Championship semifinal (the movie has it as 10 and 8). In the film Cary Middlecoff and Demaret visit Hogan while he is recovering from his car accident.

"Look, Ben, we're leaving in September to play in the Ryder Cup," says Demaret. "We want you to captain our team." Then as Demaret is leaving the hospital room he turns to Anne Baxter, playing Valerie Hogan in the movie, and says, "Bye, Val—you're looking prettier than a June bug."

In the May 4, 1951 issue of *Golf World*, Demaret proclaimed: "Take it from me, Palm Beach are the greatest slacks I've ever worn." A magazine advertisement for the fabric Orlon in 1954 explained "Why Jimmy Demaret designs his own sportshirt with Orlon." It was noted that "It washes easily, dries fast without any need for blocking. And it's out-of-bounds to moths." *Golf Digest* in its May 1954 issue showed Demaret modeling a shirt bearing his own brand. This time the shirt was made of "Thalspun, a new fabric that looks like wool and wears like iron."

All through the 1950s Demaret appeared in ads for First Flight golf balls, a company in which he had an investment. The ads proclaimed the merits of the ball's "Steel Power Center," which was meant to help balance the ball in flight.

The 1953 World Championship of Golf at Tam O'Shanter Country Club offered the largest single purse for a winner of a tournament at the time. Demaret had finished second in the 1951 playing of the event, and after he came in ninth at the 1953 tournament, he was asked into the broadcast booth to provide commentary on the finish. It was the first nationally televised PGA Tour event, which reached 646,000 television sets. One camera set behind the 18th green provided the only view of the golf course. Demaret's commentary was for the radio coverage of the tournament.

As the final twosome approached the tee at 18, Lew Worsham in that group was trailing Chandler Harper by one shot, and Worsham had to make a birdie on the par-4 hole to tie. Harper seemed so certain to win the tournament that he was being congratulated just off the back of the 18th green. Worsham's drive left him with a 123-yard approach shot to the green.

Demaret expressed doubt that Worsham would even birdie the hole, then watched Worsham's ball land short of the green, roll across it, and go straight into the hole for an eagle two and the win. Demaret blurted out to the nation's golf fans, "The sonofabitch holed it."

The first season of the *I Love Lucy* Lucille Ball television series was 1951. The show went on the air in October that year and quickly became the most popular show on television. At the time there were only three national television networks and the impact of any successful program was that much greater because there were so few choices.

Demaret appeared as himself in the May 17, 1954 episode of the show, with the situation for the particular episode being that Ricky and Fred want to discourage Lucy and Ethel from taking up golf. In order to do that they create a ridiculous series of instructions and rules for the game, resulting in Lucy and Ethel taking, on one hole, a 26 and a 30, respectively. Demaret comes along as a single and discovers Lucy and Ethel playing by themselves after being left behind by Ricky and Fred. The ladies convince Demaret to join their group and then they try to instruct Demaret in the ways of golf as told to them by their husbands. After Demaret informs the ladies that they've been duped, he plots with them to get back at Ricky and Fred. The final scene has Demaret doing a hop, skip, and jump prior to trying to hit his drive, an original preshot routine that Demaret executes very well.

Early in the *I Love Lucy* episode Ricky is seen holding a copy of Demaret's book *My Partner, Ben Hogan* that had been published in the spring of 1954. Demaret worked on one book in his life and it was somehow fitting for such an outgoing person that the subject would be someone else. The book was credited as being written with the help of Jimmy Breslin and Harry Grayson, and it was published by McGraw-Hill. The book was excerpted in the April 2, 1954 issue of *Collier's* magazine, a national general interest periodical similar to the *Saturday Evening Post*. Two years later in *Golf Digest* the book was still available as part of that magazine's Golf Library, and it sold for $2.95.

Hogan had won three professional majors in 1953, still a remarkable accomplishment. He had entered only six events for the year, still enduring the effects to his health from his car wreck of 1949, and yet he won five of them. Hogan and Demaret had partnered for six four-ball victories on the PGA Tour and in the foursomes for the Ryder Cup. In the book Demaret discussed his friendship with Hogan. "Certainly on the golf course, Hogan is a grim-faced, tight-lipped automaton," Demaret wrote. "But take it from someone who knows him well—he is also a fine, courageous, and warmhearted human being." Demaret made a definitive appraisal of Hogan's playing ability: "To my mind, Ben Hogan is the greatest golfer that ever lived, and I don't have to go far to get a lot of people to back me up."

Since Hogan won the British Open in July 1953 and Demaret's book appeared only eight months later, there must have been a feverish push to get the work done. Demaret discusses his relationship with Hogan; a bit about the history of the game of golf; the early days of the PGA tour; the two comebacks made by Hogan, one from lack of success on tour and the other from his car accident; life on the tournament trail; partnering with Hogan to win four-ball events; the dynamics of Hogan's play; and Hogan at Carnoustie, the site of his 1953 British Open victory. However it was accomplished, something of Demaret's sense of humor and good spirits come through in the book. He also manages to provide a portrait of Hogan that is respectful of his accomplishments in golf, but even more appreciative of Hogan's integrity and the seriousness with which Hogan played golf. In that focus on playing at his best Hogan may have had more in common with Demaret than most people appreciated, other than those people who knew Demaret well, and knew golf well enough to have an educated opinion about his playing ability.

In the June 1956 *Golf Digest* cover story on him, Demaret's then current noncompetitive activities were reported. "Lately Demaret has been making instructional shorts for television consumption, and spices up the presentations by interviews with such personalities as Bing Crosby, Ted Williams, Bob Hope, and leading golfers." These shows were also made available as films for rent.

One television appearance for Demaret during the 1959 television season was on the *Tonight Show*, the talk show hosted at that time by Jack Paar. The show had debuted in September 1954 with Steve Allen as host, who stayed until January 1957. Then Jack Paar took over.

Demaret had become host in 1959 of *All Star Golf* on the ABC television network and stayed with the show through 1961. The show began as a regular televised series of golf matches in 1957. A different host was used for each of the show's first two seasons. The format of the show was essentially what the later program *Shell's Wonderful World of Golf* would become in the 1960s. Two players from the PGA Tour would compete in a stroke play match. Because the matches were filmed for later airing they could be edited and condensed to show just the highlights.

In a preview of the 1960 season for the show in the November issue of *Golf Digest*, the production details for the program were discussed. "While the viewer sees 'only' 51 minutes of action on every show, an actual total of about 312 man-hours goes into just the filming of an 18-hole production."

When Demaret became a cohost of *Shell's Wonderful World of Golf* for the 1967 season he started to travel over 80,000 miles a year in order to film the matches at the various sites around the world. He would be so busy with preparations for the filming that he wouldn't take his golf clubs with him on the trips. Gene Sarazen, his cohost for the show, would play when they traveled.

"Sarazen didn't miss playing a single course we visited," said Demaret when asked about the show after his first season. "I always walked around a course at least once to become acquainted with the layout so I would know what was coming up when we shot the show. But I spent most of my time sightseeing."

Demaret joined the program for its film schedule in 1966, with his first shows airing in early 1967. *Texas Magazine*, a supplement to the *Houston Chronicle*, ran a feature by Dick Peebles on the show in February 1967.

"The crew was made up of 44 technicians and an administrative staff. Twenty-one wooden packing crates were required to hold 4 1/2 tons of equipment," wrote Peebles. "All travel was via regularly-scheduled flights on DC-8s or 707s as nothing smaller could carry the load in one hop.

"The crews required 30 single rooms with bath and five doubles at each stop. Under ideal conditions the entire crew was able to stay at the same hotel. Usually, though, crew members had to separate, sometimes in as many as nine locations. On shooting days, the crew had to be on the course at 5:30 a.m. in order to be set up for the 7:30 a.m. tee off."

One of the endorsements Demaret and Burke made together was in 1960 when they appeared in an ad for the Cushman Electric Golfer, which was the golf cart being used at Champions. Another ad in which they both appeared was for De Soto Lakes Golf and Country Club in Sarasota, Florida. Demaret was identified in the ad as president of the club and Burke as vice president. The ad ran in 1957, prior to their announcement of their plans for Champions Golf Club. Another ad the two appeared in was for Norelco dictating equipment.

"Sting Stopper," an ointment which offered "quick, temporary relief from stinging and biting insects and irritating plants when used as directed," was another product that Demaret endorsed and he appeared on the point-of-sales pieces for the product. An ad for Kodel fabric featured Jimmy in a golf shirt made of the fabric. In an ad for Equitable Life Assurance Society of the United States, the headline read, "Will he master the wind like Jimmy Demaret?" The ad featured a drawing of Demaret after his golf swing follow-through and a young boy swinging a club superimposed over that.

One of the more unusual product endorsements for him was "Jimmy Demaret's Dart Golf," which was exactly as it sounds, a dart game based on golf. Three golf holes were depicted on the dartboard: a par 3, 4, and 5. The object was to accumulate as few points as possible by hitting the appropriate target areas. Hitting the clubhouse with your dart resulted in the highest single score.

Chrysler Imperial automobile ad.

Sting Stopper point-of-sale piece.

During the summer of 1963, Demaret and Jack Burke tried to get approval from the United States Corps of Engineers to build a 36-hole golf course complex. The golf courses were to be part of a 1,000-acre section of 27,000 acres of federal land set aside for Harris County parkland. After many presentations to county officials and several years of analysis about the best plan of action, the county leased 1,641 acres from the federal government for its park, with Jay Riviere in May of 1966 ultimately winning approval of his proposal to build the golf courses, not Demaret and Burke.

Demaret's announcing at the Masters in 1962 had an influence on the outcome of the event, according to Arnold Palmer in his book *A Golfer's Life*, written with James Dodson. In the fourth round,

Will he master the wind like Jimmy Demaret?

When a strong wind blows, they call it a "Jimmy Demaret day." With good reason. For no one ever played the wind with the skill of the genial golfing great from Texas. Three-time winner of the Masters, Jimmy Demaret is now a member of the Professional Golfers' Hall of Fame.

Not every youngster can be a Jimmy Demaret. In fact, very few even participate in organized sporting events much less become stars. But every young person—if only a spectator—can be as physically fit as the most talented athlete.

Our national leaders have stated that physical fitness, particularly the fitness of our young people, has never been more important than it is today.

To support the national fitness program, Equitable has prepared a special film: "Youth Physical Fitness —A Report to the Nation." If you would like to borrow a print of this film for showing to community groups, contact your nearest Equitable office or write to Equitable's home office.

Ad for Equitable.

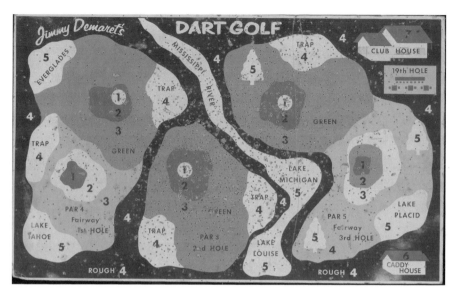

Jimmy Demaret's Dart Golf Game.

Palmer came to the par-3 16th hole trailing leaders Gary Player and Dow Finsterwald by two shots, after having started the day in front by two shots himself. An opening nine hole 39 had dropped him back. At 16 another wayward shot of the sort that had plagued him the whole day left him with a 45-foot chip shot.

"As the gallery was being moved and I stood looking over my dismal situation with disgust no doubt showing on my face," Palmer said, "I happened to overhear on-course commentator Jimmy Demaret remarking to his audience that I faced a nearly impossible shot, that I'd be extremely lucky just to get down in two. The much-needed birdie was unthinkable. 'This shot will perhaps put Arnold Palmer out of contention for the Masters Championship.'

"I think I turned and looked at Jimmy wearing a little smirk of exasperation. I can tell you his comments really revved me up inside, and when I chipped the ball into the hole and the crowd went crazy, I felt a rush of adrenaline that seemed to have been missing all day long. The charge was now on, in my mind. At 17, I made a 20-footer for a birdie and at 18 I missed my birdie attempt and had to settle for par. The Masters Championship had its first-ever three-way tie."

In winning the 18-hole play-off the next day Palmer would birdie four of the first five holes on the back nine. He shot a 68 to Player's 71 and Finsterwald's 77.

Filming the matches for *Shell's Wonderful World of Golf* took Demaret all over the world during the 1960s. He had traveled extensively before that time, winning the 1941 Argentine Open, regularly playing in Havana, Cuba, participating on the Ryder Cup team when the matches were held in Great Britain, touring Australia with other PGA Tour professionals, and traveling for many exhibition matches and for personal trips.

"I've played all over the Far East, Europe, Great Britain, all the countries of South and Central America, in Mexico, Canada, France, and Japan," Demaret said of his travels. "Wherever you go, in the richest country in the world or the poorest, you see golf being played. The game has afforded me the opportunity to meet many wonderful people. I consider it the most international game in the world."

CHAPTER 8

Onion Creek and the Legends of Golf

"A Magnificent Course in All Respects"

◆ ◆ ◆

As with the founding of Champions Golf Club, Onion Creek in Austin was a collaborative effort. Austin businessman Jimmie Connolly and Demaret announced in September of 1969 that they had assembled 750 acres of land, three miles of it along Onion Creek, in order to build a golf course and a residential home community. Other investors joined them in the enterprise, including Lumbermen's Investment Corporation of Texas.

In the book *Champions Golf Club: 1957–1976,* Demaret recalled course construction techniques he witnessed while working for John Bredemus on the building of Westwood and Brae Burn in Houston in the late 1920s.

"You should have seen how they built tees and greens in those days," Demaret chuckled. "Any dirt-moving work had to be done with a team of mules, for there were no bulldozers available at the time. At least Mr. Bredemus didn't have any. The mules pulled what was called a 'Fresno.' It was a metal bucket, and somebody had to hold onto the handles and drive the mules. When the bucket was full of dirt, they drove the mules to the spot where the dirt was to be dumped and the bucket was tilted over. Then they'd go back and get another load."

When Demaret was working on the design for Onion Creek he created the area for each sand bunker by laying out a rope on the ground to show the contours, as described earlier by Ben Crenshaw. He achieved excellent results with his somewhat primitive methods. Golf course architect Tom Fazio visited Onion Creek for the spring 1979 Legends of Golf event in which his uncle George was a participant. He wrote Demaret a letter praising the course design. "I would like to congratulate you on such an outstanding job of design and construction of the Onion Creek course," Fazio wrote. "It is a magnificent course in all respects. The variety of holes, the character of the greens, the placement of hazards create a totally overall super course." George had competed against Demaret on the PGA Tour, and had a hand in the design of the Jackrabbit course at Champions.

The Grand Opening for the golf course at Onion Creek in June of 1974 may have been part of the inspiration for the Legends of Golf tournament because several of the participants in that event participated in the opening festivities. One fivesome at the opening contained Jack Burke, Mickey Mantle, Darrell Royal, Tennessee Ernie Ford, and Willie Nelson. Burke made a hole-in-one on the second hole of the round.

Jay Hebert, who had won The PGA Championship in 1960, said of the course after playing it that day, "It's not too short if you add 20 yards here and 30 yards there. It could hold a pro tour event. It's very tight and very demanding and has small greens, but when you get the back tees, it'll be about 6,708 yards."

Another stimulus for the Legends of Golf Tournament came from a discussion between Gene Sarazen and Fred Raphael, who had been the producer of the television show *Shell's Wonderful World of Golf* during the 1960s. Sarazen was the show's original host and then he was joined in 1966 by Demaret. The show ran through the 1970 season.

"The year was 1963," recalled Raphael. "The location: the Masters in Augusta, Georgia. I was having dinner with Gene Sarazen. I asked the Squire what time he was teeing off on Saturday and who was he playing with. As he was unsure, he got up and called the clubhouse. As he returned to the table, he had a great big grin on his face. He said, 'Tomorrow, the old legend, Gene Sarazen, tees off with the future legend, Arnold Palmer.'"

Raphael had been producing televised golf matches for years, so that was nothing new to him. He was also familiar with the generation of players who had been prominent in the 1950s through the 1960s, because those were the players who had appeared on *Shell's Wonderful World of Golf.* After that show went off the air, he began to consider how he could bring back some of these players who he knew could still play competitive golf, even though competing against the younger players on the PGA Tour didn't make sense. He began having discussions with Demaret and Sarazen about the appropriate format that could feature these legends of golf.

Raphael finally got NBC interested in the concept, but the network wanted a live event, not the filmed format of *Shell's Wonderful World of Golf.* The question then became could the players, some of whom had not played tournament golf in many years, play at a level that would be appealing to golf fans? The answer was yes.

For the first event, Sam Snead was partnered in the two-man, best ball format, with Gardner Dickinson. Snead birdied the 16th and 17th holes to tie the Australian team of Peter Thompson and Kel Nagle. Then, on 18, Snead put his wedge shot just four feet from the pin and Snead made his third straight birdie to win the event. He and Dickinson each made $50,000 in winning the first Legends of Golf.

"Golf fans still wanted to see their heroes play golf," said Jack Treece, the superintendent at Onion Creek at the time. "Here were these guys that could play great golf, but they didn't have anywhere to play, and the people who had seen them during their glory years missed them and wanted to see them tee it up again."

Demaret understood the appeal of the format and the participants. "I would guess that 95% of the golfers in the world today," said

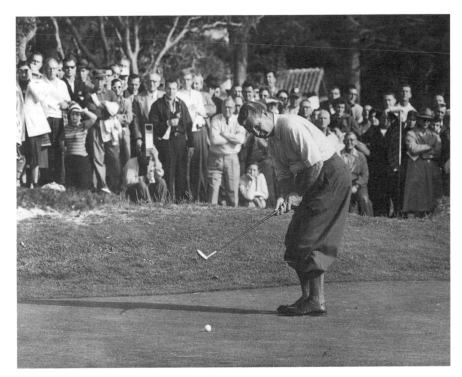

Demaret often played in plus fours in his later years. (courtesy of The PGA of America)

Demaret in 1979, "most members of country clubs, and those between the ages of 40 and 65, associate with the men in this field more than they do with a majority of the players on the tour."

By the late 1970s golf clothes for all players had become colorful and Demaret no longer stood out as the one bright spot on a course. He remembered how he had first arranged to have custom golf clothes made for himself in his early days as a professional golfer. "In 1938 or 1939 I had a deal with Palm Beach (clothing manufacturers) and I went to New York City to have some nice outfits made," said Demaret. "They sent me to a tailor, Harold Dryer. I still remember the address—545 Fifth Avenue. He started showing me the blue and brown materials, and I pointed toward some other stuff across the store. They were bright colors. He said, 'That's material for women's clothes. You can't have clothes made from women's material.' I said,

'The hell I can't. Make 'em.' I then got pieces of the material and sent them to a shoemaker in Brockton (Mass.). He put a saddle on all of my shoes, using the material. I had the first color shoes to match golf clothes."

In reminiscing about his early days on tour, Demaret recalled the influence that Walter Hagen had on him. "I'll admit I tried to be like him," said Demaret. "He was a very natty dresser, although they didn't have colors then. I remember seeing him drive up in a limousine, get out and go to the tee. We had some times together right at the end of his career. Walter and I did a little partying together."

Several of Demaret's celebrity friends participated in the first Legends of Golf tournament, including Bob Hope and Phil Harris. Demaret's long association with Hollywood was a unique aspect of his career. "I played golf with so many of the big stars," said Demaret. "I spent a lot of time with Laurel and Hardy and Adolph Menjou. I played golf with Bogart."

"I could only have met these people through golf. No football player or baseball player can get close to people through the playing of their game. Golf brings people together like no other sport."

The 1979 Legends of Golf tournament regulation play ended in a tie between the team of Roberto de Vicenzo and Julius Boros, and the team of Tommy Bolt and Art Wall. The play-off went to six holes, with de Vicenzo and Boros winning. The tournament's extended play put the program into prime-time viewing and the audience response made it clear that golf fans wanted to see more. This got the interest of the PGA Tour, which began formulating plans to develop more events featuring the older players, and thus was born the PGA Senior Tour.

Liberty Mutual Group became the title sponsor of the event in 1980 and that gave the tournament a solid financial backing. Fred Raphael would later credit the support of Liberty Mutual for sustaining the event when it needed help. Their support has continued since they got involved in 1980. Another major development for that year was that Arnold Palmer became eligible to participate and his

*Demaret with Phil Harris. The photograph is inscribed to Curtis Wilson,
Charlie Wilson's son. (courtesy of Curtis Wilson)*

presence added another strong dimension of fan interest. He had been a crowd favorite since winning the Masters in 1958 more than 20 years before. The PGA Senior Tour had two events that year, five the next, and now, as the Champions Tour, it has more than 30.

Darrell Royal, who as coach of the Texas Longhorns won two national championships in football, moved to the Onion Creek home community after he retired from coaching. His home was next door to Demaret's partner in the development, Jimmie Connolly. The Royal home at Onion Creek had a basement den that had an old style potbellied stove in it, which behind it had a tile heat guard along the wall. The stove was never used, but Demaret signed one of the tiles.

In that basement several of the after-hours celebrations were held during the week of the Legends of Golf tournament when Larry Gatlin would perform in Royal's den and Demaret would sing harmony. "I can't imagine Jimmy Demaret with anything other than a smile or laughing," said Royal. The two would play golf together at Champions when Royal would visit Houston.

For one of the first Legends of Golf tournaments Royal was matched with Gene Sarazen as the honorary starters for the event. When they finished their round they were more than four holes ahead of the next group. "This is the way I like to play golf," Sarazen told Royal after they had played a few holes. "You don't waste any time."

Royal also had the opportunity to play golf with Ben Hogan. Fran Trimble in the May 2001 issue of *Golf Houston Magazine* told a story about the round Royal had with Hogan: "Once, when Darrell Royal was playing a round with the great Ben Hogan, the football coach hit his tee shot into fairly deep woods. Royal and Hogan both went to where the ball lay in jail and Royal selected some kind of long iron for a heroic attempt. The great Hogan grumped, 'You practice that shot much?' Royal never said a word, but put the club back, took a 7-iron and punched sideways out of the woods and back to the fairway."

For the final round of the 1980 Legends event, Demaret and Gene Sarazen showed up late for their tee time, thinking that they were to start at 11 a.m., as they had for the previous day's round. Sarazen arrived soon enough to join his partner Jim Ferrier on the first tee, and apologized to everyone. Demaret was so late that he had to catch up after the first hole. "It's embarrassing," Demaret said at the time. "That was the first time in my career that I have missed a tee time. I was up at daybreak and was reading the paper. I thought they were going to use the same starting time as Saturday, 11 o'clock. Nobody ever said we were going to start earlier." When Demaret finally caught up with his group he had to play in street shoes. The tee time change had been made as an accommodation to the television broadcast of the event.

After hosting the event for its first three years there was discussion that the event would be moved to another site. The issue was primarily that the show's producer, Fred Raphael, wanted a $50,000 guarantee from the club. He had also become interested in raising the prize money from a total purse of $400,000 to $500,000. The success of the event, and the response from the television audience, created growing pains for the tournament. All was finally resolved and the event remained at Onion Creek until 1990.

The worthiness of the format, and the appeal to golf fans of seeing some of the great players of the game continue competing, are evident in that the Liberty Mutual Legends of Golf is still being played and is successful. Lee Trevino for 1990 won more money as the leading money winner on the then-PGA Senior Tour than did the leading money winner on the PGA Tour, Greg Norman.

Demaret's friend Charlie Wilson organized a plan to have a bust created of Jimmy that could reside at Onion Creek in honor of his contributions to the club. The bust was placed on July 4, 1984. Forty-four contributors made donations toward the creation of the bust. Among them were Miller Barber, Tommy Bolt, Gene Cernan, Ben Crenshaw, Charlie Crenshaw, Jay Hebert, Kel Nagle, Bob Rosburg, Mike Souchak, Peter Thompson, Jack Treece, Lee Trevino, Curtis Wilson, Charlie Wilson, and Ken Venturi.

In 1993 Fred Raphael influenced the naming of the Demaret Division for the Legends of Golf tournament. Several of the players who had participated in the inaugural event in 1978 could no longer

Bust of Jimmy Demaret at Onion Creek. (courtesy of Charlie Wilson)

compete with the younger players, and the format had been changed from two-man teams to an individual winner for the overall event. The new Demaret Division included players age 70 and older, still competing in the two-man team format.

CHAPTER 9

THE DEMARET LEGACY

"In the Spirit of Fun"

◆ ◆ ◆

W hen he was given the Walter Hagen Award for 1974, the citation read, "Jimmy Demaret has not only enhanced the golfing game through his skills, proven by his triumphs in the world's
major golf tournaments, but he has also enlivened it through his
warm, engaging personality. Like Walter Hagen himself, Jimmy
Demaret has shown us that the sport of golf can rise beyond being
merely an athletic event into an occasion and opportunity for building goodwill and friendships among peoples of varying backgrounds
and nationalities."

The Walter Hagen Award is annually given to the golfer or golf
executive who does the most to further good relations in the sport
between the United States and Britain. It is named after the first winner, Hagen, who was the 1961 recipient of the award.

Demaret is mentioned in several books that list or rank the top
players in the game's history. Robert McCord in his book *The Golf
100: Ranking the Greatest Golfers of All Time* developed an interesting methodology of determining who were the best players in history.

1. Relative standing of the golfer in his era.
2. Number of significant championships won, starting with
the majors.

3. The strength of the field.
4. Awards won, such as Player of the Year; leading money winner; the Vardon Trophy for lowest stroke average; and honors such as selection to the Ryder Cup team.
5. Contribution to the game.

In the first category, comparing Demaret to Nelson, Hogan, and Snead may seem to diminish his accomplishments, because these men achieved so much. Snead still has the most total PGA Tour victories at 82. Hogan won three majors in 1954 alone and 64 tour events in his career. Nelson won 11 tournaments in a row (actually 12—one of the events he won in 1945 didn't have the $3,000 total purse necessary to qualify as a tour event), and a total of 52 events on tour, despite retiring relatively early at age 34. Competing against some of the greatest players the game has known and winning 31 tour events, including three Masters, actually seems more impressive.

As for winning significant championships, Demaret was the first golfer to win the Masters three times, and at age 52 in 1962 he could still accomplish a fifth place finish. While he didn't win any other majors, he did win all six of his matches in his Ryder Cup team participation, still the only undefeated record of anyone who has competed in at least six matches.

The strength of the field, or what was the quality of the competition that Demaret faced, is answered by the first criterion. In his era Demaret competed not only against Nelson, Hogan, and Snead, but also Horton Smith, Craig Wood, Lloyd Mangrum, Ralph Guldahl, Paul Runyan, Henry Picard, Cary Middlecoff, Harold "Jug" McSpaden, Bobby Locke, and Tommy Bolt among others.

As for awards, Demaret in 1947 won the Vardon trophy, the leading money winner title, and was named player of the year. He was named to four Ryder Cup teams, beginning with the 1943 team that did not play against a team from Great Britain, and then 1947, '49, and '51, winning all his matches as stated above. He was inducted into all the significant halls of fame in golf, including The PGA, World

Demaret was presented with head covers made of mink by Bing Crosby in 1952. (courtesy of Alex Morrison)

Golf, Texas Sports, and Texas Golf Halls of Fame. McCord, in *The Golf 100,* ranks Demaret at number 19.

Robert T. Bruns in his entry on Demaret for the *Scribner Encyclopedia of American Lives* gives an assessment of Demaret's stature among PGA Tour players. "Demaret's place as a golf talent is defined by the tour rankings of the PGA Tour statistical project in 1989, which compiled the records of nearly 4,000 players from 1916 through 1988," wrote Bruns. "The statistics concentrated on performance in significant events rather than money won. In percent of purse from 1916 to 1988 Demaret ranked twelfth; using the Ryder Cup point system he ranked ninth; and in lifetime points he ranked thirteenth. He was the winner of 31 official PGA Tour tournaments and 43 tournaments overall."

Asian Golf Monthly magazine ranked all golfers in 2002. Their methodology included awarding points for various categories of achievement; for example, 1,000 points for each major won, 375 points for each PGA tour victory, 500 points for a Vardon Trophy, etc. After compiling all the points Demaret ranked number 27.

Reid Spencer in the book *Sporting News Selects the 50 Greatest Golfers* places Demaret at number 29. While no rigorous methodology is explained in the book, the usual accomplishments seem to figure in the book's rankings, including number of majors won and number of overall victories.

Demaret reduced his play on the PGA Tour in 1958 to just a few tournaments. His standing among the all-time money leaders up to that point provides another measure of how well he played, especially considering that to earn money in the early days of the PGA Tour meant finishing among the top 20 players. Through 1957, Demaret was the sixth leading money winner. Leading the list was Sam Snead, followed by Ben Hogan, Cary Middlecoff, Lloyd Mangrum, and Byron Nelson.

As for his contribution to the game of golf, many people consider Demaret someone who dramatically increased the spectator appeal for the professional tour from the late 1930s into the 1950s. Prior to the television era, which did not begin for golf coverage un-

Demaret in his later years. (courtesy of The PGA of America)

til the mid-1950s, PGA Tour events often struggled to attract spectators. Combined with his tour wins, the founding of Champions Golf
Club, which has hosted many significant events over the years, and
his entertaining demeanor, Demaret can be seen to have contributed as much as anyone in the game during his era, and maybe all
who followed him.

Demaret was celebrated on many occasions during his life, several of them large programs, such as the 1951 dinner in New York
arranged by Toots Shor referred to in Chapter 3. One recognition
that shows how highly he was regarded as a competitive golfer was
given him in 1952 when he was named to the PGA's Mid-Century
Honor Roll of Golf "by the golf professions and sports press of the
nation as one of the 10 outstanding professional golfers of the last 50
years."

In his *The Swing's the Thing* golf instruction set in 1959, Demaret wrote about how much this particular award meant to him. "Receiving this award provided me with one of the most wholly satisfactory and proud moments of my life. Not so much because a group of men decided that I am one of the 10 outstanding professional golfers of the past 50 years, but mostly because the award was voted to me by professional golfers and professional sportswriters who have dedicated their working lives to the game which is my professional life."

What Demaret had accomplished as a golfer would not be something the average player could expect to experience, which he understood. Demaret then described how he recommended that the average golfer would best enjoy the game. "Golf is a game. If you're going to get the most out of it, you should approach the learning of it and the playing of it in the spirit of fun and not as if you were a scientist studying the game through a microscope. You can spend only so much time practicing. In the long run it's the amount of time you will be able to devote to the game that will determine your ability to play it well. There is no other way. So relax while you're learning and while you're playing. If you do, this great game of ours with its etiquette, tradition, and challenge, will treat you as it's treated me ... as the game of a lifetime."

In January of 1960, Demaret and Ben Hogan were named cochairmen of the Texas Heart Fund campaign for the year. In November Demaret joined Bob Hope, Jerry Lewis, Mickey Mantle, and Jack Burke in a fund-raiser for the campaign, a nine-hole outing that attracted a gallery of 3,000 spectators. In October 1960 Demaret was inducted into the PGA Hall of Fame along with Mike Brady, who twice lost in play-offs for the U.S. Open, in 1911 and 1919, and Fred McLeod, who won the U.S. Open in 1908 by defeating Willie Smith in a play-off. A year later Demaret was inducted into the Texas Sports Hall of Fame.

More than 500 people attended the Interfaith Charity Bowl banquet on December 2, 1962 that honored Demaret as Mr. Sportsman of the Year. In his opening remarks to the crowd at the banquet Demaret said, "I have never known persons by their religions, only

The Demaret swing. (courtesy of The PGA of America)

by their names." Among the people sending congratulatory telegrams were Ben Hogan, Bobby Jones, Arnold Palmer, Mickey Mantle, Perry Como, the Ames brothers, Bing Crosby, and Demaret's fellow Texan and U.S. vice president Lyndon Johnson. As part of the ongoing festivities, the following Sunday during halftime of the Houston Oilers-Denver Broncos game, Demaret was again honored.

Dick Peebles in the *Houston Chronicle* noted that Toots Shor was the featured speaker for the evening. "Referring to Demaret's choice of loud, colorful clothing, Shor recalled the words of the late Bugs Baer after first seeing Jimmy on a golf course, 'He looks like lightning striking a paint factory.'"

On February 14, 1977, Demaret was the guest of honor for the World Championship Toast and Roast Dinner at the Shamrock Hilton benefiting the Houston Association of Big Brothers. Houston city councilman Louis Macey proclaimed it Jimmy Demaret Day in the city. The Houston Sportswriters and Sportscasters Association organized the event attended by more than 900 people that also honored the outstanding athlete of 1976, an award won by Tommy Kramer, Rice University quarterback. Many of Demaret's celebrity friends turned out to help roast him, including Phil Harris, former Houston Oiler football team executive John Breen, radio personality Paul Berlin, and astronaut Gene Cernan, with Dave Marr serving as master of ceremonies. Jack Agnes in the *Houston Post* told some of the remarks made at Demaret's expense.

"Golfer Ken Venturi said he remembered a time when the driest place on Monterey Peninsula was Jimmy Demaret's martini glass."

Agnes quoted Jack Burke Jr. in the article: "Jack said he was tired of hearing about Demaret's humble beginnings. 'After all of his stories about selling newspapers on Christmas Day, there is a lot of casual water in our office.'"

In May 1983 Demaret was inducted into the World Golf Hall of Fame. Bob Hope, who had partnered with Demaret several times for the Pro-Am of the Crosby Pebble Beach event, was inducted at the same time, with Hope and Crosby being the only entertainers honored by inclusion in the Hall.

At the time the World Golf Hall of Fame was located at Pinehurst, North Carolina. As part of the induction activities Demaret played golf on Pinehurst No. 2 with Bob Hope, Gene Cernan, and Alan Shepard. *The Houston Chronicle* reported that Demaret's attire for the round included "a bright apricot sweater, white knickers, argyle socks, and orange and black golf shoes."

The Memorial Tournament in Columbus, Ohio for 1990 had as its honoree Jimmy Demaret. The tournament was founded by Jack Nicklaus in 1976 with four major objectives: further the game of golf; to remember and honor great golfers of the past; to stage the finest possible golf tournament for his hometown of Columbus, Ohio; and to benefit local charities. Every year the tournament selects a golfer whose accomplishments are celebrated during tournament week.

In describing Demaret's impact on the game of golf the Memorial Tournament said of him: "Although one of the finest players of his day, the winner of three Masters tournaments (1940, 1947, and 1950) among his many tour victories, Demaret's contribution to golf may be most pronounced as a promoter of the game. With the inherent showmanship of the nightclub singer he always wanted to be and the inveterate charm of the born bon vivant, Demaret brought flair and flash to every stop the tour made. Playing and socializing with Hollywood movie stars like Bing Crosby, Bob Hope, Johnny Weissmuller, and Randolph Scott, Demaret helped give the tour glamour and high-profile celebrity. He provided the game a media spotlight.

"He spent his career advancing the game and the game is better for his participation in it. Jimmy Demaret, the 1990 Memorial Tournament Honoree, will be remembered as a good friend of golf."

Ben Hogan's assessment of his four-ball partner may have been the most credible judgment of Demaret's playing ability.

Hogan: "He was the most underrated golfer in history. This man played shots I hadn't even dreamed of. I learned them. But it was Jimmy who showed them to me first."

Demaret made contributions to the game in many different ways. His personal generosity is less well known. There were many people

Demaret was the honoree at the Memorial Tournament in 1990. (courtesy of the Memorial Tournament)

during his life who benefited from introductions he made, job opportunities he identified, and business deals in which he allowed his friends to participate.

Frances Trimble, in a 2001 article in *Golf Houston Magazine,* quoted Demaret's friend A.J. "Bones" Maloney, who first met him in 1934 when Demaret played in the Texas PGA in Dallas. Maloney moved to Houston in 1937 and lived near Brae Burn Country Club where Demaret was head professional at the time. Maloney recalled how Demaret after World War II still remembered what it was like to be a caddie. "Just before Christmas, we'd drive around to all the Houston golf courses—there were only about six at that time—and he would open his trunk and give bottles of cheer to all the caddies."

Johnny Silva was 13 years old in 1951 when he first met Demaret. He met Mahlon Demaret before he met Jimmy while Johnny was working as a caddie at Golf Crest Country Club in Houston. Mahlon was working at the club as an assistant pro and during the school year, when Silva worked from 4 p.m. until closing, Mahlon would give Silva a ride home from the club due to the curfew for teenagers in the city at that time. It was through Mahlon that Silva met Jimmy, which after Silva's time in the service led to a job opportunity at Champions in 1958.

In 1962 Silva became the head professional at the Valley Inn Country Club in Brownsville, Texas at the southern tip of the state, through an introduction made by Demaret. Jimmy and his friends would fly down to play golf and go fishing. Several years later, in the mid-1960s Silva was brought to the Concord Hotel where Jimmy was the touring pro. Silva would work from March into September at the resort. Jimmy would visit the property usually for a weekend or other brief stays.

Silva recalls being in New York in the '60s, having lunch one time with friends at Minucci's restaurant, a favorite hangout of golf professionals in the metropolitan area. On that day Silva did not realize that Demaret was also in the restaurant. The waiter appeared at Silva's table with a $50 bill and said to Silva, "That man over there said to give you this to pay for your lunch, but if you eat more than this will cover, you've got to pay for it yourself." When Silva looked across the restaurant, there was Demaret, grinning as usual.

Through Jimmy, Silva met George Fazio, who designed the Jackrabbit course at Champions Golf Club. During the 1970s Silva worked for George Fazio in course construction work across the U.S., and he and Jimmy spent a lot of time together in Houston from 1974 until Jimmy passed away in 1983.

One night when the two of them were in a bar they frequented Jimmy discovered that one of the patrons was there celebrating a birthday. Jimmy stood up and proclaimed that for entertainment in honor of the birthday, the crowd would be enjoying Johnny Silva sing, much to Silva's surprise. But he got up, sang a song to everyone's delight, and then sat down again. He was astonished that Jimmy wasn't the one who sang, and he asked him, "Jimmy, you're a much better singer than me—why didn't you sing?" Jimmy replied, "They couldn't afford me."

Chilly Newman, who was friends with Demaret from the early 1940s through the rest of his life, recalled meeting him at Brae Burn Country Club at a fund-raiser for the war effort. Newman was 12 years younger than Demaret. Later both of them moved their families to northwest Houston, and Newman eventually became a member at Champions.

"Jimmy had a fantastic memory," said Newman. "He told me one time that he made more money knowing people's names and knowing people than he did on the golf course. He didn't mean it per dollar, but he meant that he built relationships."

After World War II, Newman came back to Houston and re-enrolled in the University of Houston, where he played on the golf team.

"During my University of Houston fame, which was only for a couple of years, we had the invitation to play at Brae Burn Country Club, Westwood Country Club, or Harvard Park," said Newman. "Well, I used to go to Harvard Park and I would skip class and hustle golf. That's where I ran across Tommy Bolt. Jimmy helped him get a car with the understanding that Tommy Bolt was to take Jackie Burke with him on the tour. Well, they started out and they didn't go very far. Tommy sold the car. He had one of the prettiest swings there ever was.

"I started Newman Supply Corporation about 35 years ago with a gentleman out of Wichita, Kansas. If either one of us did anything wrong the other could buy him out. This fellow didn't do right, so I decided to buy him out. So I was making an arrangement through the bank for a loan. Jimmy and I were drinking a beer at the Red Baron, one of our usual drinking spots. And he said: You're going to do what? I said, I'm going to borrow money to make a down payment and buy this thing out. After a couple of beers he says, I want that loan. I said if you're serious, you meet me next morning at First City National, I'll ask the banker about it. Jimmy said: I'll be there. Jimmy got on the elevator with me the next morning. He had on purple shorts, purple socks, white shoes, purple shirt. When we sat down with the banker, Jimmy took a check out of his pocket and smoothed it out and wrote me a check for $50,000. I paid him back in 5 years with interest."

"One time Jimmy took me over to the Masters. Mike Souchak and Nancy, and Jack Burke and Ilene, and Jimmy and Idella rented a house. This was years ago. Mike had a deal with Oldsmobile and I had the car and I would pick them up in the morning and I would take them to the Masters and drop them off prior to their tee times. This particular time Jimmy had me registered as his son-in-law. I was at the course one day and I saw Mr. Jones was out on a concrete bench by himself underneath a tree. He kind of waved at me, so I went and sat down with him. We talked about 15–20 minutes. His hands were so gnarled. He couldn't hardly get his hand loose. He knew what the hell you were going to say before you said it. He was really bright. He figured out real quickly that I wasn't named Walter Jackson, but Chilly Newman."

Newman became close to many members of the Demaret family and hosted a reunion of both families several years after Jimmy died. He was the person who broke the news to Idella, Jimmy's wife, that he had died while at work at Champions on the morning of December 8, 1983.

"When Jimmy Demaret died, Jimmy Burke, Jack Burke Jr.'s brother, called me and had me go tell Idella. So I went up to the door and I knocked. She said: What are you doing here this early? I said I've got some bad news. We've lost Newt [James Newton Demaret's nickname]. She shut the door and wouldn't let me in. She cried. Sort of semiscreamed. After she did let me in, I was monitoring the phone calls, of course. And one of the first calls they got was Mr. Hogan. He couldn't handle it. He couldn't stand it for maybe a minute. Valerie Hogan, Ben's wife, came on the phone and wanted to know if she could speak to Idella. I said, absolutely, of course. So I went to the back of the house and told her Mrs. Valerie Hogan was on the phone and could she talk. Idella said, yes, I'll talk. But Mr. Hogan couldn't handle it."

Dave Marr recalled Jimmy Demaret in the program for the 1990 Memorial Tournament, which featured Demaret as the event honoree that year.

"I go all the way back to the earliest childhood with Demaret," said Marr. "My mother and dad used to double date with Jimmy and Idella when the guys were young single pros growing up in Houston. I didn't see much of Jimmy during the war because he was in the service. After the war, I really got to know him. My dad died in 1948 and Jimmy always kinda took care of me. When he'd come to Houston, he'd ask me to caddie and give me $10 when the caddie fee was $3. Golleee, that was big!

"The thing about Demaret that was wonderful: up to his dying day, he was one of those people you were always glad to see, because there was a warmth, a charisma there.

"When you were with Jimmy, it was good times, and good things happened. He was always good for a story or a laugh. He got along with everybody and I never heard him say a bad thing about anybody. He genuinely cared about people.

"The night of Jimmy's wake in Houston, Phil Harris came in and he got to telling stories. We were all laughing and crying, standing outside the church. You'd have thought it was a bunch of hysterical drunks, and nobody had even had a drink—yet. Jimmy would have been proud."

Marr also spoke of Demaret in an interview with Peter McCleery in *Golf Digest* that appeared in the September 1997 issue. "Demaret never said anything bad about anybody. He turned everything into a positive, happy moment. You were always glad to see Jimmy coming. He was a Hagenesque kind of guy, a good-time Charlie. But Jimmy couldn't have done what he did and misbehaved that much. He loved movies, he loved football, he loved life, he loved people. If things got tense, he left. He wasn't about to put up with any bull—. He would sit and drink with you and laugh and solve the problems of the world, but you were not going to talk about anything serious."

After Demaret died in 1983, Hogan composed a letter to him, a tribute to their friendship, which was read at the memorial service for Demaret at Holy Rosary Catholic Church in Houston on January 6, 1984.

> To Jimmy Demaret, My Dear Friend and Playing Partner:
>
> I know you are here with us today in spirit for this deserving effort in your honor. Your warm and happy smile can be seen and felt by everyone present.
>
> As partners, you and I never lost a four-ball match and, although I will be a little tardy in joining you, I want you to keep practicing so that one day we can win another four-ball together.
>
> I send to you my admiration and thanks for all the nice things you have done for me and others—you helped make my bad times more bearable and my good times better. You were my friend and I miss you. May you sleep in peace and I will join you later.

HIGHLIGHTS OF DEMARET'S PLAYING RECORD

◆ ◆ ◆

Victories

1934 — Texas PGA (won this event four years consecutively) *
1938 — San Francisco Match Play Tournament
1939 — Los Angeles Open
1940 — San Francisco Match Play
　　　　Oakland Open
　　　　Western Open
　　　　New Orleans Open
　　　　St. Petersburg Open
　　　　The Masters
1941 — Inverness Four-ball (w/ Hogan)
　　　　Argentine Open *
1946 — Inverness Four-ball (w/ Hogan)
　　　　Tucson Open
　　　　Miami Four-ball (w/ Hogan)
1947 — The Masters
　　　　Tucson Open
　　　　St. Petersburg Open
　　　　Miami Four-ball (w/ Hogan)
　　　　Miami Open
　　　　Inverness Round Robin Four-ball (w/ Hogan)
1948 — Inverness Four-ball (w/ Hogan)
　　　　Albuquerque Open
　　　　St. Paul Open
1949 — Phoenix Open

1950 — Ben Hogan Open
        Atlanta Open
        The Masters
1951 — Havana Pro-Am Invitational *
1952 — Bing Crosby Pro-Am Invitational
        National Celebrities Open
1953 — Thunderbird Invitational
        La Gorce Pro-Am *
1956 — Thunderbird Invitational
1957 — Thunderbird Invitational
        Baton Rouge Open
        Arlington Open
1961 — Canadian Cup (w/ Snead) *

* Not an official PGA Tour Win

Runner-up

1940 — Inverness Invitational
1942 — Hale America Tournament
1945 — Glen Garden Invitational
1946 — Jacksonville Open
        Charlotte Open
        Atlanta Open
1947 — Atlanta Open
        Richmond Open
        San Antonio Open
        Columbus Invitational
        Albuquerque Open
        Orlando Open
1948 — Richmond Open
        Phoenix Open
        Texas Open
        Rio Grande Open
        U.S. Open
        Dapper Dan Invitational

1949 — Long Beach Open
       World Championship of Golf
1950 — Texas Open
       Greensboro Open
1951 — World Championship of Golf
1952 — San Diego Open
       Mexico City Open
1953 — Palm Beach Round Robin
1956 — Labatt Open
1959 — Bing Crosby Invitational
1964 — Palm Springs Golf Classic

Tied for Second

1956 — Baton Rouge Open
1957 — Tournament of Champions
1958 — Thunderbird Invitational
1959 — Thunderbird Invitational

Other Achievements

Ryder Cup: 1947, 1949, 1951 - Record: 6 wins, no losses - best winning percentage in Ryder Cup play for all participants with at least 6 matches

PGA Championship: Quarterfinalist — 1948
                          Semifinalist — 1942, 1946, 1950
Masters: Champion in 1940, 1947, 1950
U.S. Open: 2nd in 1948, T-4 in 1953, 3rd in 1957
British Open: Tied for 10th in 1954

Jimmy Demaret finished in the money in over 325 tournaments during his playing career.

ACKNOWLEDGMENTS

My first phone call to begin work on this book was to Tad Weeks, who has served as head professional at Champions Golf Club in Houston, Texas, for more than 20 years. Tad introduced me to Jack Burke, he put me in touch with many of Jimmy Demaret's friends, and he provided me with some of the preliminary materials I used in my research. Tad's encouragement and cooperation guided me throughout this whole process.

I would also like to recognize Jack Burke and his entire staff at Champions, including Shirley Sembritzky and Shawna Wallstein, who assisted me at various stages in the book's development. Jimmy Demaret's family was also quite helpful, and I want to thank his daughter Peggy, his siblings Jane and Mahlon, Mahlon's wife Mercedes, and Jimmy's nephew Tracy Demaret.

Jimmy Demaret's friends who helped include Ray Ayles, Gene Cernan, Ben Crenshaw and his agent Scott Sayers Jr., Earl Elliott, Eddie Merrins, Byron Nelson, Charles Newman, Harold Norman, Darrell Royal, Louise Suggs, Jack Treece, Charlie Walling, Charlie and Connie Wilson, Charlie's sons Curtis and Cary Wilson, and the staff at Onion Creek Golf Club. They all provided valuable insight into Jimmy's life.

Among my fellow golf writers there were many who assisted me, including Jim Apfelbaum, Al Barkow, Furman Bisher, Dan Jenkins, Russ Pate, Lorne Rubenstein, and Curt Sampson. Special thanks have to go to Fran Trimble, formerly the curator of the Texas Golf Hall of Fame and a writer on the game for 20 years. Her bio reads: "As a child, she attended many professional tournaments with her parents during a time when tour pros were just people and not rock stars. She played in her first tournament at age eight, losing to a boy who is now a major beer distributor in South Texas. Since older family members played golf and talked golf, the game's 'schtick' rubbed off. She started writing golf in 1984 and before that was a medical writer and technical writer."

Research assistance was provided by Lauren Cobb, Julius Mason, Bob Denney, and Rebecca Szmukler at the PGA of America; Patty Moran and Doug Stark of the U.S.G.A.; Mike Waldron and the Georgia State Golf Association; Gary Fisketjon; Richard and Betty Lewis; Gene McClure; Vicki Ellis at Brae Burn Country Club; Elmer Stephens; Rice University; the Collections in the Center for American History at the University of Texas at Austin; the Memorial Tournament; the Jack Nicklaus Museum; the Houston Public Library; the *Dallas Morning News;* the *Houston Chronicle; Golf Digest;* Atlanta Public Library; Emory University's Robert W. Woodruff Library; Historic Golf Photos; Associated Press; David Wigner; and Martha Heagany at Barton Creek Club and Resort.

To everyone who provided assistance to me, my thanks.

OTHER GREAT GOLF TITLES FROM CLOCK TOWER PRESS

Golf Books as Timeless as the Game

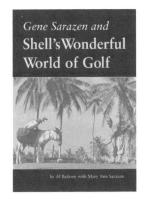

Gene Sarazen & Shell's Wonderful World of Golf
by Al Barkow and Mary Ann Sarazen
$29.95

A behind-the-scenes look at television's first major golf show from one of the original writers, and the daughter of golfing legend Gene Sarazen.

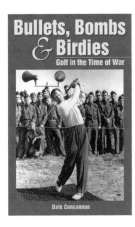

Bullets, Bombs & Birdies: Golf in the Time of War
by Dale Concannon
$19.95

Ever since the game began, golf and war have been oddly connected. Read about golfers who let nothing—not mortar shells, the threat of gas attacks or even incarceration in a POW camp— get in the way of a round of golf.

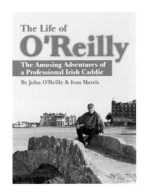

The Life of O'Reilly: The Amusing Adventures of a Professional Irish Caddie
by John O'Reilly & Ivan Morris
$10.95 (softcover)

Take a rollicking ride around the world—and the world of professional golf—with one of the game's most interesting characters, caddie John O'Reilly.

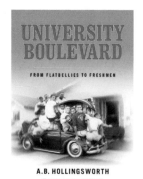

University Boulevard
by A.B. Hollingsworth
$22.95

A sequel to the best-seller *Flatbellies*, the close-knit group of "golfing misfits" now enters college during the turbulent times of the Vietnam War.

Golf Nuts: You've Got To Be Committed
by Ron Garland
$18.95

All golfers are at least a little nuts about the game, and because of that, every golfer will be able to relate to these zany antics of the members of the Golf Nuts Society as told by founder Ron Garland.

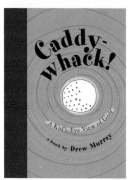

Caddywhack! A Kid's-Eye View of Golf
by Drew Murray
$14.95

Discover that a golf course is not just for golf, that there is a community of golf, that there are hazards to avoid and what are the most important things in golf. As a parent, you will learn about how to let kids enjoy a sport for what it is, from their perspective—a kid's-eye view. And then just get out of the way.

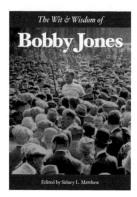

The Wit & Wisdom of Bobby Jones
by Sidney L. Matthew
$14.95

Sportsmen continue to marvel that Bobby Jones's legacy remains unparalleled in golf history. One of the reasons why is because Jones was more than the consummate champion golfer. This collection of quotes captures his spirit.

Corporate and volume sales are available for all titles. Please call 1-800-956-8999. Clock Tower Press, 3622 W. Liberty, Ann Arbor, MI 48103, www.clocktowerpress.com, www.huronriverpress.com.